CARADOC JONES
A FORGOTTEN MISSIONARY

CARADOC JONES
A FORGOTTEN MISSIONARY

*The life and work of
Caradoc Jones, Rhosllannerchrugog*

NOEL GIBBARD

Printed by Gwasg y Bwthyn, Caernarfon

CONTENTS

ACKNOWLEDGEMENTS

During my research for this work, I had the opportunity to meet a few people that knew Caradoc Jones: the late Edna Evans, né Jones, Ponciau, Rhosllannerchrugog, Caradoc Jones' niece; Mrs Sylvia Le Saux, Reading; Mr and Mrs Havard Gregory, Cardiff, and Beryl Hall, Cardiff; who provided me with much information, and took me around Rhosllannerchrugog to see places of significance in the life of Caradoc Jones. Dr Phil Ellis, Mrs Gill Burns, Mrs Siân Thomas and Mrs Cutts, all from Cardiff, also helped me. My sincere thanks to all of them.

A brief visit to Paimpol was a means of capturing the atmosphere of the place, and at the church the family appreciated the welcome of M. Garsmeur and his friend. The Rev. Michael McGowan, a former pastor at Paimpol, and Mr John Emyr, Cardiff, most kindly read the work and encouraged me to publish. The Pioneer Mission Collection is kept at the Angus Library, Regent's Park, Oxford, and I am grateful to Mrs Mills, the Librarian, for her welcome and help during my visits to Oxford. I would like to acknowledge copyright holders for permission to publish: The National Archives, Kew, for including material from Home Office and Foreign Office Collections; Mr G. Constable, Orpington, Kent, and the Imperial War Museum for quoting from the 'Diaries of Miss M. Bayliss'.

Financial help was received from the trustees of the Cardiff City Mission that made it possible to publish this work. I am most grateful to them for their support. Once again I am indebted to Mr Edmund Owen for preparing the Index. Thanks are due to the staff of Gwasg y Bwthyn for their diligence and patience in preparing the work for the press.

Cardiff   *NOEL GIBBARD*

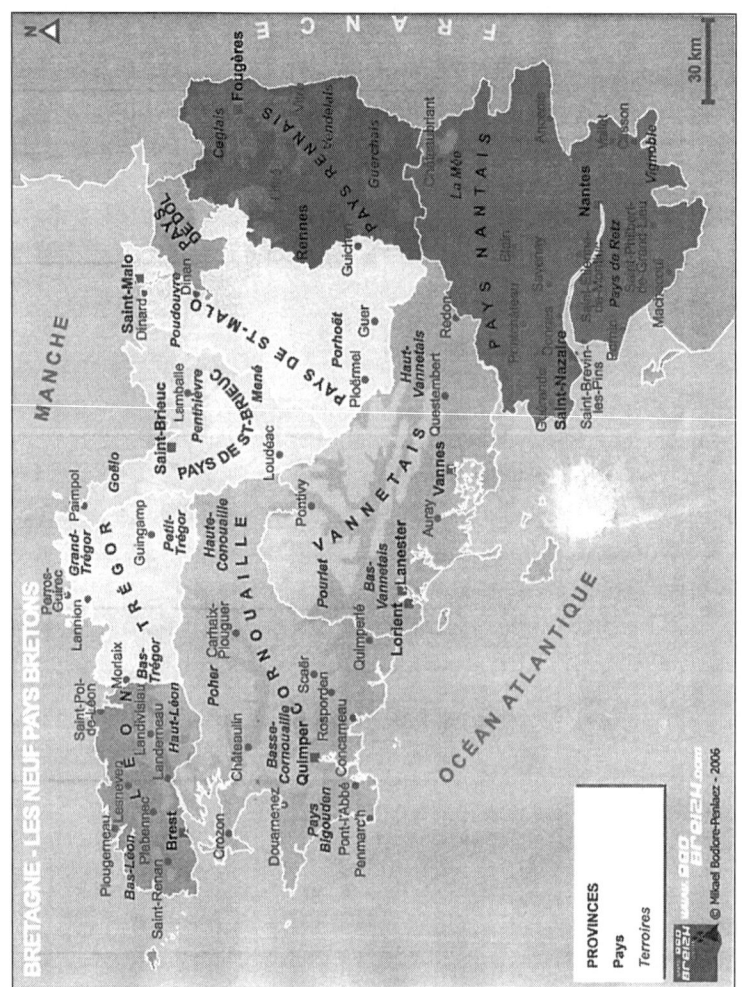

Brittany Provinces.
(From geobreizh.com by permission of Mikael Bodlore-Penlaez)

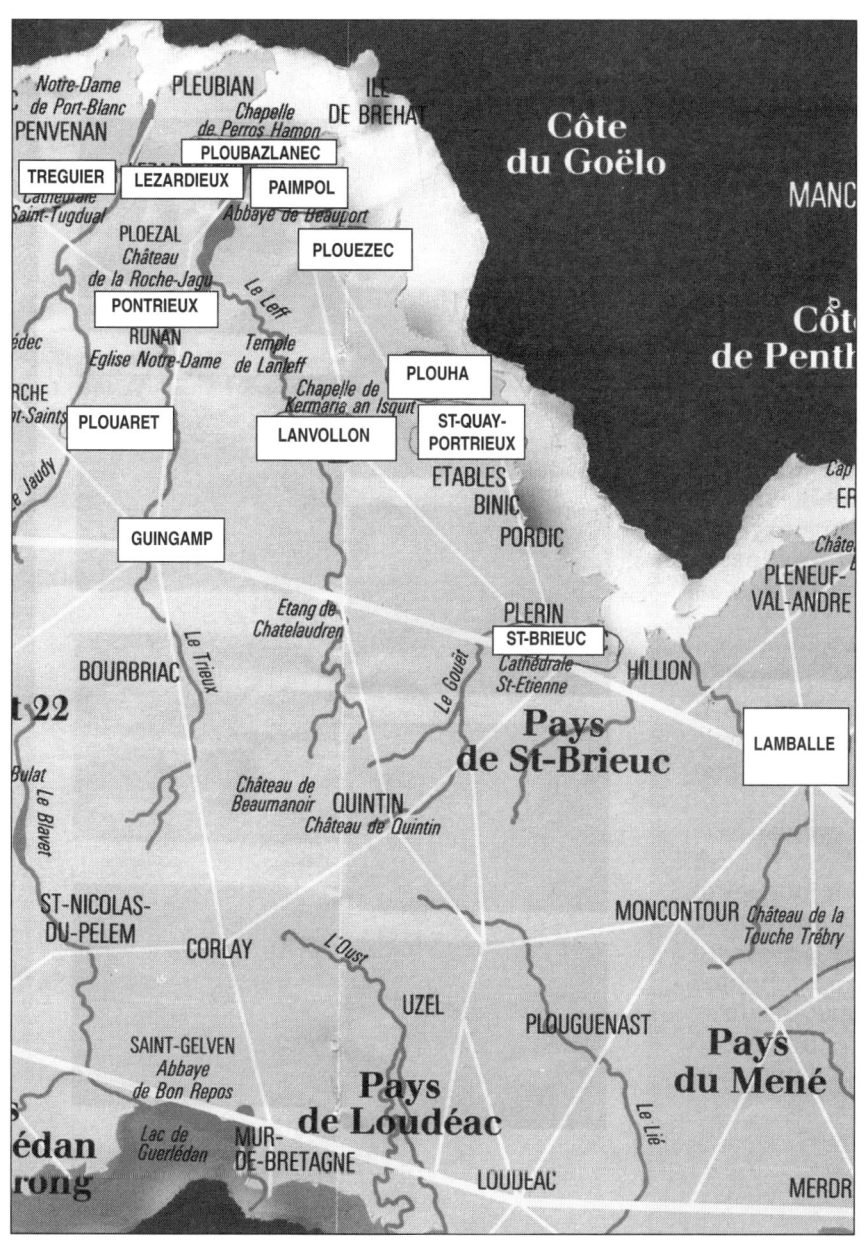

Map showing Paimpol
and some of the places in which Caradoc Jones worked

1

WELSH RHOS AND SCOTCH BAPTISTS
1875-1901

Caradoc Jones was a young man in his early teens. An elder in the Pontfadog Scotch Baptist church, Glyn Ceiriog, Denbighshire (Clwyd) asked him to take the reading and the prayer in one of the services. The young lad was quite surprised with the request but did not like to refuse. He had a little time to prepare before the service and took part rather hesitantly and nervously.[1] The event made a lasting impression on him. It made him more seriously minded and more concerned with spiritual matters. Caradoc Jones was from Ponciau, Rhosllannerchrugog (Rhos), four miles from Wrexham and eight miles from Pontfadog. The family belonged to the small Scotch Baptist denomination in Rhos and had links with Pontfadog.

RHOS
Rhosllannerchrugog (Rhos) was clustered with places of worship when Caradoc Jones was born 2 January 1875. Most of them are still there, but are far from being as full as they were just over a hundred years ago. At the beginning of the twentieth century, a small area like Ponciau, had seven chapels, five belonging to the Baptists, of which three were Scotch Baptists and the Congregationalists and Calvinistic Methodists had one each. All seven were Welsh language causes and the only English cause was Mount Pleasant Baptist church. Other English causes were located in Rhos itself, the Primitive Methodists, the Salvation Army and the Anglican Church that arranged some Welsh services.[2]

It was in such a religious society that Caradoc Jones was born. The outlook on life was predominantly religious. The chapels were the main centres of attraction, with the Bible governing the worship and thinking of their people. There was, also, a general respect for religion. Usually, whole families attended Sunday worship, as was true of the Jones family, which was comprised of William and Maria, the parents, and the five sons, Frederick, Henry, Caradoc, William Stephen and Stephen David.[3] Sunday worship would be part of the family piety: 'He [Caradoc Jones] grew up in a home where the piety of the parents made a deep impression on their children'.[4] Sunday was respected generally, but Sabbatarianism could be burdensome for the children. An inhabitant of Rhos, reminiscening on his childhood, could remember the occasion when he picked some flowers on Sunday as a little present for his parents. When he arrived home he was severely reprimanded and told to throw them away.[5] Culturally, the main events were the eisteddfodau, that is, competitive meetings, and performances by the choir. Much tension was felt among the eisteddfod competitors. They could be jealous of each other and critical of the judges, who, in the opinion of the competitors, were very often biased and unjust in their remarks. Cultural events took place in the chapel and at least one chapel had an annual eisteddfod on Easter Friday.[6] The furtherance of Welsh culture was regarded as part of the chapel's mission.

Music played a significant part in the life of Rhos. It was bound up with piety. A singing school had been started there as early as 1829 to teach 'the principles of singing and religious music'.[7] A class to learn sol-fa was formed in the 1860's. The first choir was formed in 1863 and one of its best-known conductors was the able musician Richard Mills. He also established the *Rhos Herald* in 1894.[8] When Richard Mills resigned as conductor of the choir, his place was taken by Henry Stephen Jones, an uncle of Caradoc Jones.[9] One of his brothers, William Stephen, married into the Mills family, and became Welsh editor of the *Rhos Herald*.[10] Such inter marriages strengthened the sense of community. Caradoc Jones himself learned to play the piano and had a good singing voice.

As in other areas in Wales, the Temperance movement had much support in Rhos. It was concerned with the effects of alcohol, and the churches bitterly criticized drunkenness and the brewers.[11] The chapel and the public house represented two different cultures. Sometimes these two cultures overlapped. Welsh Societies and Friendly Societies usually met in public houses and chapel-goers and non-chapel goers could attend their meetings. A Welsh Society met in the White Horse and each person was allowed a maximum of four pennies worth of drink. It was open to all kinds of people.[12]

The people of Rhos could pay money into a Friendly Society and benefit when there was a time of illness. They could also benefit from a 'Clwb Arian' (Money club) or borrow money and pay a five per cent interest.[13] It was in such a way that many families bought their own home, rather than living in a rented house. It was quite a change for a large family living in a two-roomed house to move into a larger home. Examples are mentioned of six to eight people living in a two-roomed house. Such a family would have been glad to share three rooms.[14]

The life of that small area reflects the industrial changes that were taking place in Rhos and district. With the increase of population many more houses were built. The building programme increased, however, without much planning. It did not matter much where the front or back door would be and it was possible to move from one house to the other either through the front or back entrance.[15] Usually there would be a pigsty at the bottom of the garden and if at all possible a family would keep two pigs, one for the family, the other to cover debts that would probably be incurred during the year.[16]

Most of the people of Rhos would find work in the colliery or the brick works. At one time there were fifty collieries and five brick works in Rhos and the immediate area. In these places of work, the cultural and industrial aspects would be brought together, as workers would discuss literary, political and religious matters. Two of the brick works were very close to the home of the Jones family. One of them was Hafod. When Hafod-y-bwch Colliery & Brickworks went into liquidation in 1879, Henry Dennis built a 'Massive new brick works south of the colliery, the site of the present day factory' (written in 2003).[17] Henry Dennis, horseman, engineer, agriculturist and county councillor, came to the area from Bodmin, Cornwall, and in a very short time he built an empire for himself. The brick works at Hafod covered an area of ten to twelve acres and employed 360 men, while the colliery employed 1,000 workers. Henry Dennis had other interests in the area apart from the colliery and brick works.[18]

In 1881, sixty-seven houses were listed for that small area of Aberderfyn, Ponciau. Seven heads of families were described as 'colliers' and five as 'brick workers', William Jones, Caradoc's father, being one of them, and he was a terra cotta packer worker. In a few years time, William David, the youngest son, joined him in that work. Included also in that area were a professor of music, a curate and Daniel Davies, 'Baptist minister and collier'.[19] One of his sons was a labourer in a brick works. In six houses a few streets away, nine of the inhabitants were colliers.[20] Added to the large number of colliers and the good number of brick workers were the small shopkeepers and the craftsmen. There was much variety within this close knit society.

Life could be very hard for the workers. A collier would work from six o'clock in the morning until half past three in the afternoon. His wage would be 3s-6d (21p) a day. A brick worker would work longer hours, from six o'clock until half past five in the afternoon. His wage would be 18s to £1 a week (95-100p) which was regarded as a living wage.[21] This was the amount that William Jones, Caradoc Jones' father, would receive as a brick maker. He would be part of a work force that included many children, who would help the older

14

workers. The owner of the works would appoint an overseer and he would be responsible for employing men, and an employee would take his own assistant, usually a boy, and he would be paid from the weekly wage. The more skilled workers would have a permanent appointment while others were employed for a brief period and even for a day. Such an arrangement created much uncertainty for the worker and his family.[22]

The weather could create a problem for the brick works. Because it depended heavily on water, drought and frost would greatly hamper the work. The works could also come to a halt because of a dispute or a slump in the industry, causing much hardship. This was the case in 1875, the year when Caradoc Jones was born: 'In 1878 there were reports of people starving in the streets as poverty caused much suffering in Rhos. In the previous three years several collieries and brick works had closed resulting in about 1,200 men being made unemployed'.[23] The unemployed found it difficult to endure during such a period, especially if the works did not provide sick benefit for its workers.

The family of the brick worker depended on coal for their fire. When it was scarce they would have to visit the colliery. The Jones family had a donkey, more for the pleasure of the children than for work, but when there was need of coal he had to be put in the harness. Members of the family would get up very early in the morning to go to the Vauxhall Colliery and take their place in the queue to reach the 'Billy', a large iron coffer with a door at the bottom. When the door opened, two persons, one on each side gathered the coal into a basket to be weighed and taken to the cart. A load of coal without dust would cost a shilling (5p).[24] There were two other aspects to the service of the donkey. The youngest of the Jones brothers was very friendly with the son of Jarvis, the policeman. Jarvis was a keen gardener and when he needed manure it was the donkey that brought it from a nearby farm. Thus the donkey linked the agricultural and industrial life of the area, because he was the one to carry manure and coal. The donkey was also, promoting good family relationships, and an added bonus was to be friendly with the family of the policeman.

The people of Rhos looked for provision for body and spirit. A local poet, writing in strict metre, made that point in one line: 'Beibl a rhaw i bobl y Rhos'[25] (Bible and shovel for the people of Rhos). Caradoc Jones' father knew how to use his hands in order to keep the family and knew that his spirit would not be fed without the Bible. Unlike the father, the son did not go to the works, but both father and son were convinced that what they needed spiritually was provided by the Scotch Baptists. It is necessary to trace the origin and development of the denomination, because several branches of the Jones family had an important role to play in its history. By the time Caradoc Jones was born, the family could already survey nearly eighty years of Scotch Baptist history.

THE SCOTCH BAPTISTS IN NORTH WALES

The year 1789 is a convenient date to begin the story. During that year a significant event took place in Maes-y-berllan, Breconshire (Powys). The Baptist Assembly was being held there, and among the representatives from north Wales was J. R. Jones, Ramoth, well known as a leader and for his warm evangelicalism. The minister and his fellow representatives from north Wales had a mission to accomplish. They were convinced that they should not return to north Wales without taking a young preacher from south Wales with them. That young preacher was Christmas Evans.[26] They presented the invitation to him and Christmas Evans responded positively. After lunch they started on their journey to north Wales. The preacher from south Wales had a preaching tour in mind, but the preaching tour led to a long stay in north Wales. Christmas Evans stayed to become, with J. R. Jones, Ramoth, the two strongest Baptist leaders in the whole of north Wales.

The Baptists did not have a real impact in the North until 1776 when Baptist missionaries from south Wales arrived.[27] By this time the effects of the Methodist Revival were also felt among the Baptists. Christmas Evans referred to the influence of Calvinistic Methodist preachers on him during his ministry in the Llŷn Peninsula. He mentioned Evan Richardson, Caernarfon (1759-1824) and even more important Robert Roberts, Clynnog (1762-1802).[28] Under their ministry, the Spirit of God humbled the congregations, but the humbling would lead to intense joy and praise when the message of salvation was proclaimed. Christmas Evans experienced the same unction on his preaching during his ministry in Llŷn.[29]

New causes were established and new preachers emerged, zealous for the proclamation of the gospel. The sun seemed to shine on the Baptists in north Wales. There was, however, a storm on the horizon. Robert Roberts, Rhos-ddu, Wrexham, introduced J. R. Jones, Ramoth, to the works of John Glass, Robert Sandeman and Archibald McLean from Scotland. Under their influence, especially that of McLean, J. R. Jones became convinced of the Scotch Baptist teaching:[30]

> In the year 1795 a considerable change took place in my religious sentiments respecting the Person and Sonship of Christ, his finished work as the only ground of hope to helpless and guilty sinners, the nature and effect of saving faith, purity and communion and order of primitive church &. The instrumental means of this important change were the writings of our beloved brother Archibald McLean of Edinburgh and his colleagues.

The main influence was McLean but J. R. Jones also mentions 'his colleagues' and the Ramoth pastor was labelled as a Sandemanian, a name he did not like.

J. R. Jones and others came to definite conclusions concerning belief and practice.[31] Each congregation should have a plurality of elders, if at all possible. They could not see any Scriptural basis for a separate, paid ministry, although it was proper to acknowledge the services of a preacher. The gospel ministry was given to the church and the minister (elder) should be set apart by the congregation. A communion service should be held every Sunday morning. The love feast should be kept; believers should wash each other's feet, and only believers should sing in public worship. Later, in the nineteenth century, disagreement arose concerning the last three latter matters.

The content of the preaching of the gospel is the revelation of God in Christ, whose finished work on the cross is the only foundation of acceptance with God. Salvation is by faith, which was defined as accepting God's witness to his Son. It was wrong, according to J. R. Jones, to look to the heart for signs of saving grace and make those signs the proof of faith. He always emphasized that it was wrong to confuse faith and the effects of faith. The basis of faith is external and is based completely on the finished work of Christ. If the effect of faith is included that gives room to boasting because it is on the basis of something the sinner himself has done. Those elected to life will acknowledge the truth, but there is a need for the aid of the Holy Spirit to believe the truth. The same Spirit will give assurance; will witness with the spirit of the believer that he is a child of God and will bring joy, hope and enjoyment of salvation.[32] J. R. Jones was strongly opposed to what he regarded as the over emotionalism of the Methodists.

For a brief period in his ministry, Christmas Evans accepted the teaching of the Scotch Baptists. He himself and J. R. Jones were the two champions of the belief in north Wales. Their influence had an impact on many churches throughout that area. For about five years, the two stalwarts worked together but the relationship was broken before the end of 1798. J. R. Jones called a meeting at Ramoth in order to find out who were standing on New Testament truth and were ready 'to leave the old Babylon'.[33] In the afternoon meeting, J. R. Jones presented detailed reasons for leaving the old Baptists. He claimed that their doctrine was corrupted and that they were unfaithful to the teaching of the apostles. Christmas Evans, although he agreed with J. R. Jones on many points was unwilling to leave the old Baptists. The pastor of Ramoth was more than disappointed that Christmas Evans would not stand with him. J. R. Jones stood up and declared publicly that he was leaving the old Baptists and joining the Scotch Baptists. Such was the emotion that some wept and others groaned. J. R. Jones and his people thought it was a Jubilee. A critic believed that they were like the thieves during the French Revolution, hoping to gain from the destruction of the city of Paris.[34]

SCOTCH BAPTIST CHURCHES

The impact of the Scotch Baptist teaching was felt before the meeting of 1798, but the division of that year opened up the way for further division, in Merionethshire, J. R. Jones' home county, Denbighshire and Caernarvonshire.[35] Caradoc Jones' forefathers were prominent in what happened in some of the churches, especially in Ruthin and Rhos, Denbighshire. In Ruthin, a division had taken place concerning the calling of a minister, and one of the men involved in the dispute was Roger Stephen, Caradoc Jones' great, great grandfather. The two Glyn Ceiriog ministers, Thomas Jones and John Edwards, had oversight of the congregation that separated to Pontgarreg. It was accepted to the Assembly at Glyn Ceiriog in 1796, when Christmas Evans and J. R. Jones were present.[36]

During the Assembly, discussions took place concerning the Scotch Baptists and disagreement was quite evident. After the meetings, tension was felt in Glyn Ceiriog itself and a split took place in Tabernacle Baptist church. Thirty-three members led by John Edwards, left because they accepted Scotch Baptist teaching, and J. R. Jones and Christmas Evans constituted them as a church. Thomas Jones remained as pastor of the old Baptist cause in Tabernacle. The two ministers had to separate and it must have had an impact on a small rural community like Glyn Ceiriog.[37]

Thomas Jones and John Edwards, Glyn Ceiriog, had taken

opposite sides in the Baptist debate. The former was determined to continue as an old Baptist, while the latter was convinced of Scotch Baptist principles. Tensions in Glyn Ceiriog were bound to have an impact on the congregation in Ruthin. Some of the members were drawn to Thomas Jones and others to John Edwards. For a while the congregation kept as one and met in different places. The inevitable happened at a communion service when Thomas Jones, an old Baptist, announced that only those of that persuasion should partake of the Lord's Supper. As a result of the announcement, 28 sat down for communion and 17 left the building. One of the 17 was Roger Stephen, Caradoc Jones's great, great grandfather and the one involved in the division of 1795. He had been a staunch old Baptist member and had welcomed the members to worship in his home. He was, now, involved in another division.[38]

RHOSLLANNERCHRUGOG AND PONTFADOG

Slowly, the Scotch Baptist churches emerged in north Wales. By the end of 1800 there were three in Merionethshire, two in Caernarvonshire and three in Denbighshire. The three in Denbighshire were Glyn Ceiriog, Ruthin and Rhosllannerchrugog. A small group met in Rhosllannerchrugog and about 1804, Roger Stephen, Caradoc Jones' great, great grandfather, moved from Ruthin and joined them. The Scotch Baptists had been meeting for a brief period in Penrhos, but had to leave because the tenant belonged to the old Baptist. The company moved into Rhos itself and met in different homes, but mainly in the home of Roger Stephen.[39]

The Scotch Baptists had two elders to lead them, Robert Roberts,[40] who introduced J. R. Jones to the work of McLean, and Robert Humphreys, but only for a brief period. Robert Roberts left for another part of north Wales and Robert Humphreys for America. He had married Mary, a daughter of Roger Stephen. One of his sons was

Stephen, who adopted Jones as the family name, and was Caradoc's great grandfather, but many members of the family kept the Stephen as well as the Jones.[41] He was noted for his kindness. It is known that on one occasion a member was taken to the workhouse, but Stephen Jones brought him back and gave him a home.[42]

Stephen Jones was working in Llangollen and it was while returning there on one occasion that he stopped to read his New Testament. The words from John 3:16, 'For God so loved the world that he gave his only begotten son that whosoever believeth in him should not perish but have everlasting life', brought him 'heavenly light'. It was as a result of this experience that he joined the Scotch Baptists at Rhos. He was appointed an elder in 1808/9.[43]

The Scotch Baptists in Rhos had no permanent building. They had to wait for eight years before they had a place of their own. Land was obtained in Aberderfyn and Soar was built in 1816. The core of the group was the Stephen family: Roger Stephen, the father, Stephen, son, John Stephen, son, Roger, son and Mary, daughter. Altogether there were nineteen or twenty members. Three of the Stephen family were also trustees and one other trustee was J. R. Jones, Ramoth. He had a continuing interest in the Scotch Baptists in the whole of north Wales until his death in 1822.[44]

Roger Stephen the father died in 1826 and was buried at the side of the chapel in Aberderfyn, which after his death was called 'Capel Rosier' (Roger's chapel). Stephen Jones, the son, was the only elder until 1834, when John Davies was appointed as another elder. Another split took place in 1840 as a result of the Campbellite teaching being introduced in 1836. Two parties were formed in Aberderfyn, the Scotch Baptists and the Campellites and both parties met in the same building. The main Campbellite leaders were John Davies, the elder, and John Williams, author of a popular book, *Yr Oraclau Bywiol* (*The Living Oracles*). He had a familiar way of presenting his message. Many would gather around him, then he, sitting on his heels, collier fashion, and, smoking his long pipe would instruct the listeners. He would allow them to ask questions at the end and endeavoured to answer them.[45]

The Campbellites agreed with the Scotch Baptists concerning the local church and the place of elders. There were, however, important differences. They were not as Calvinistic as the Scotch Baptists and wavered between moderate Calvinism and Arminianism, but three things in particular, differentiated them from the Scotch Baptists. First of all, they believed that the moral law of the Old Testament applied to Jews and that it had no demand on Christian believers. Secondly, baptism was considered within the process of conversion. It was thought of in terms of repentance, new birth but that spiritual experience could not be enjoyed without baptism. The teaching could easily give the impression that baptism was necessary for salvation. Lastly, although they acknowledged the significance of preaching, nothing could be compared with the experience of partaking of the Lord's Supper. It was a memorial, a spiritual experience and it was, also, the most effective way of preaching.[46]

Matters came to a head in 1840. John Davies and his people left the church in Aberderfyn. This must have been a matter of great sorrow because two elders had chosen to part, and, also, two of John Davies' sons were apprenticed with one of the Stephen family who was a cobbler. There is no doubt that the division affected the growth of the church. This is reflected in the figures for 1836 and 1851:[47]

1836	1851
20	morning 7 afternoon 24
	Stephen Jones, minister

Numerically, little progress had been made during a period of fifteen years. Glyn Ceiriog had succeeded in keeping a steady attendance of 60, while the numbers at a new cause at Pontfadog varied between ten and twenty-five.[48] The members met in a small building, 'Yr Herber', before moving into the village itself in 1892, but occasional meetings were still held in the original home.[49] Members of the

Stephen/Jones family continued to minister at Rhos, in Soar, Aberderfyn and at Tabernacle, Rhos, when it was opened.

William Jones, Caradoc's father, was made an elder at Pontfadog, eight miles from the home of the family.[50] On a Sunday, the son would accompany the father to Pontfadog. In the early days there were only two meetings, morning and afternoon. Sometime, it is not known exactly when, an evening meeting was added. Morning would be devoted to prayer and exhortation, the Lord's Supper would be administered in the afternoon and the evening service set apart for preaching the gospel. Between the morning and afternoon services the members gathered for a Love Feast, 'when they partook of the food they had brought along, bread and cheese being a prominent item'.[51] Father and son would walk a mile to a member's home for tea and walk back to Aberderfyn after the evening service. Monday morning, the father would be up early to go to the brick works.

It was at Pontfadog that Caradoc Jones was asked to read and pray in one of the services. About the same time he came under conviction of sin, but it is not clear if this happened at Pontfadog, although the report seems to take for granted that it was at that place. Henry, one of the brothers, was already converted; Caradoc was concerned about his salvation and that of one of his other brothers, Frederick. Caradoc Jones went to hear Samuel Pierce, one of the Scotch Baptist preachers:[52]

> His theme was the angel's message to Lot, 'Escape thou for thy life; look not behind thee neither stay thou in the plain'. In graphic language he described the calamity that overtook the inhabitants of Sodom, and the terrible danger to those who dallied on the plain. Under the solemn warning, as the story was applied, people were broken down in repentance, and among those that wept were Caradoc and his eldest brother, and William who was two years younger. Then the preacher spoke

of Zoar, the place of safety, using it as a picture of Christ, the eternal refuge of the soul.

As a result of that meeting, seven souls found refuge in Christ. Three of the seven became preachers of the gospel and all of them remained faithful to the Saviour to the end of their days.

It was some time before Caradoc Jones' vocation came clear to him. When he was fifteen years of age he was apprenticed to a grocer in Wrexham and had experience of town life and people. He stayed there during the week and returned home for the weekend. This meant that he missed the mid-week meetings but continued to benefit from the Sunday services.[53] After three years in Wrexham, Caradoc Jones settled in Rhos and opened a little shop of his own in Craigfryn, the family home. As a result of his return it was possible for him to have closer fellowship with his fellow Scotch Baptists. The shop brought him into close contact with the villagers. The children were regular customers, and on a Monday morning, Caradoc Jones would ask them for the verse they had learned on the Sunday. Every child that could recite a verse received some sweets.[54] The number of verses recited in the local chapels must have increased considerably during this time.

Caradoc Jones was not just concerned with the number of verses that the children knew; he wanted them to have Scriptural knowledge. He himself, at a young age, was well versed in the Scriptures and church meetings confirmed his desire to know them even better. He also took part in the services, including the Society meeting. As he was nurtured at home and in the church, the young man had a desire to preach. His first sermon was based on the story of Naaman the Syrian, especially the words 'Go again seven times'. It was not the last time for him to preach that sermon.[55]

After starting to preach, Caradoc Jones could have continued as a preacher and probably would have been made an elder, but some events were to change the course of his life. Before the end of the nineteenth century, efforts were made to unite the old Particular Baptists and the Scotch Baptists. Marked progress was made, but a few among the Scotch Baptists in Gwynedd were strongly opposed to such a move. They gained the support of the church at Rhos. In a meeting to discuss the possibility of unity, most of the Scotch Baptists were represented, including Pontfadog, but Rhos and a few others refused to join. Rhos opposed the move, but Stephen Jones, Caradoc Jones' uncle, who ministered in Porthmadog, was part of the discussions. There was a difference of opinion within the family.[56]

Caradoc Jones himself was greatly concerned as he believed that the attitude of the Rhos brethren was narrow. The two Baptist denominations did agree on principles of co-operation and not union. They agreed to co-operate in areas where there was no Baptist church and that weekly communion would be celebrated in that new cause.[57] Tensions continued in Harlech and Rhos. The angular attitude of his own people grieved Caradoc Jones. Another event was to force him to reconsider his place within the Scotch Baptist denomination.

1. Winifred M. Pearce, *Knight in Royal Service* (Pioneer Mission, London, 1962), 9.
2. D. Myrddin Davies, 'Cyfnodau a Digwyddiadau', *Bedyddwyr Rhosllannerchrugog, 1789-1989* (Rhosllannerchrugog, 1989); Rhosydd Williams, *Hanes Rhosllannerchrugog* (Rhosllannerchrugog, 1945), 15-6.
3. Ruabon, Census Returns, 1881.
4. *Knight in Royal Service*, 7.
5. William Phillips, *Atgofion* (Caernarfon, 1955), 84.
6. *Hanes Rhosllannerchrugog*, 23-4.
7. Ibid. 25..
8. For Richard Mills (1840-1903): *Dictionary of Welsh Biography down to 1940* (London, 1959), under his father, Richard Mills (1809-44). [*DWB*].
9. A tribute to him: 'Crefyddol a chyffredinol', *Yr Ymwelydd*, June 1915. One of the speakers at the meeting was the musician Caradog Roberts, Rhos. Henry S. Jones contributed hymn tunes to *Yr Ymwelydd*, e.g. 'Bryn Maelor', February 1900; 'Cymdeithas', March 1900; during the War period: 'Mons', January 1915; 'Antwerp', May 1915.

10. 'Death of Mr. W. S. Jones', *Rhos Herald*, 24 August 1963; account of the funeral, 31 August 1963. William Phillips, *Atgofion*, 5.
11. *Hanes Rhosllannerchrugog*, 29.
12. Ibid. 23.
13. Ibid. 29
14. William Phillips, *Atgofion*, 5.
15. Ibid. Census Returns, 1881.
16. *Hanes Rhosllannerchrugog*, 30.
17. Andrew Connolly, *Life in the Victorian Brickyards of Flintshire and Denbighshire* (Carreg Gwalch, 2003), 234-5.
18. Ibid., and photograph, 235; T. W Pritchard, *Remembering Ruabon/Cofio Rhiwabon* (Ruabon and District Field Club, 2000), 150-1, and photograph, 150.
19. Census Returns, 1881, 1901.The two sisters, Mrs Beryl Hall and Mrs Myfi Cosslett, Cardiff, are descendants of Daniel Davies, and related to Caradoc Jones. His mother, Maria, né Davies, was the daughter of Dafydd Dafis and Margaret, the daughter of Stephen Jones, first minister of Soar: Family Tree, presented by Mrs Beryl Hall, Cardiff.
20. Ibid.
21. William Phillips, *Atgofion*, 6, 23. 'We worked from 6 in the morning until 5.30 in the afternoon, five days a week. On Saturdays we finished at one o'clock. Our programme never varied. On Mondays and Tuesdays we made floor-tiles, bricks and drainage pipes; on Wednesdays we emptied one of the two kilns. On Thursdays we filled it up again, this generally lasting a week', T. W. Pritchard, *Remembering Ruabon*, 150.
22. Connolly, *Life in Victorian Brickyards*, 55.
23. www.bbc.co.uk/wales/northeast viewed 21/12/04.
24. W. S. Jones, 'Y Llyn Mawr ac Aberderfyn', *Rhos Herald*, 16 February 1963.
25. *Hanes Rhosllannerchrugog*, 9.
26. John Richard Jones (1765-1822), *DWB*. Christmas Evans (1766-1838): D. Densil Morgan, *Christmas Evans a'r Ymneilltuaeth Newydd* (Gomer, Llandysul, 1991); Tim Shenton, *Christmas Evans* (Evangelical Press, 2001); *DWB*.
27. T. M. Bassett, *Bedyddwyr Cymru* (Swansea, 1977), 95-101.
28. Shenton, *Christmas Evans*, 104-5, 108-9.
29. D, Densil Morgan, *Christmas Evans*, ch. 3; Shenton, *Christmas Evans*, ch. 8.
30. David Williams, *Cofiant J. R. Jones, Ramoth* (Carmarthen, 1913), 691.
31. Ibid. ch. XXII.
32. Ibid.
33. D. Densil Morgan, *Christmas Evans*, 42; David Williams, *Cofiant J. R. Jones*, chap. XVIII.
34. D. Densil Morgan, *Christmas Evans*, 43.
35. Shenton, *Christmas Evans*, 493 (37) gives a list of 9 Scotch Baptist churches; it is, therefore, an exaggeration for him to say that 'churches all over the North followed his lead', 163.
36. J. Spinther James, *Hanes y Bedyddwyr yng Nghymru* (Carmarthen, 1903), vol. III, 459.

37. Ibid., 461-2; J. D. Davies, 'Hanes Bedyddwyr Albanaidd a Champbelaidd yng Nghymru', *Trafodion Cymdeithas Hanes y Bedyddwyr*, 1940; 'Adgof Uwch Anghof', *Yr Ymwelydd*, August, September, 1896.
38. Spinther, *Hanes y Bedyddwyr* vol. 111, 461-2.
39. J. D. Davies, 'Hanes Bedyddwyr Albanaidd a Champbelaidd'; Spinther, *Hanes y Bedyddwyr*, vol. IV (Carmarthen, 1907), 93.
40. D. Densil Morgan says that nothing much is known of Robert Roberts, *Christmas Evans*, 36, but there are references in Spinther, *Hanes y Bedyddwyr*, vol. III, 325, 360.
41. J. D. Davies has an account of Stephen Jones' life: 'Adgof uwch Anghof', *Yr Ymwelydd*, August-November 1896.
42. Ibid., October 1896.
43. Ibid., September 1896.
44. J. D. Davies, *Trafodion Cymdeithas Hanes y Bedyddwyr*, 1940.
45. Ibid., the section 'Campbeliaeth yng Nghymru'.
46. Ibid.
47. Ieuan Gwynedd Jones, ed. *A Calendar of Returns Relating to Wales* (Cardiff, vol. 2, 1981), 154.
48. Ibid., 246.
49. Dewi Parry Jones and Robert Owen Jones, *100 Years in the Valley* (Ceiriog Press, 1999), 122, with photograph; T. Frimston, *Dewi Mawrth a'i Amserau*, (Blaenau Ffestiniog, 1924) 161-2.
50. William Jones, died 30 January 1935: 'A daeth i ben deithio byd', *Yr Ymwelydd*, February 1935. Maria, his wife, died 18 April 1924: *Yr Ymwelydd*, August 1924. Stephen Jones, Caradoc's grandfather ministered at Porthmadog; two uncles, Stephen and James in Rhos; two brothers, Henry and William Stephen in Rhos and another brother, Frederick, at Glyn Ceiriog. Because Soar was small, Tabernacle was opened in 1884, Denbigh Record Office, NTD/713, extracts from *Yr Ymwelydd*, June 1883, April 1884.
51. *Knight in Royal Service*, 8.
52. Ibid., 9.
53. Ibid.
54. Recollections of Mrs. Edna Evans, né Jones, Caradoc Jones' niece, Ponciau. Rhosllannerchrugog. In 1901, Caradoc Jones is described as 'Grocer shopkeeper'; Henry as 'House painter & Decorator'; William as 'Printer Compositor', and Stephen as 'Terra Cotta Presser', Census Returns 1901. Frederick is not included; by this time, probably, he had moved to South Bank, Yorkshire
55. *Knight in Royal Service*, 9.
56. 'Y Bedyddwyr Neilltuol', *Yr Ymwelydd*, July, August, September, 1880; Ibid. 'Cyfarfod o Gynhadledd y Bedyddwyr Albanaidd, Harlech, Mai 7ed 1894', October 1894; D. Davies, *Cofiant y Diweddar Hybarch Morris Rowland* (Llangollen, 1899), ch's. X, XI, XII.
57. Ibid., 88-90.

2

COLLEGE AND REVIVAL
1901-7

In no time Caradoc Jones became a popular preacher. He was prominent in evangelistic meetings arranged by the Scotch Baptists. For example, Caradoc Jones, his father and a few other Scotch Baptists were involved in a series of evangelistic meetings from the 25 February to the 11 March 1901.[1] He received invitations to preach with the Old Baptists and the Primitive Methodists as well as the Scotch Baptists.

DENOMINATIONAL ALLEGIANCE
The fact that Caradoc Jones accepted invitations from other denominations was frowned upon by many within the Scotch Baptist churches. The feeling was so strong that they asked the young preacher to sign a written declaration to the effect that he would not preach in other denominational churches. Caradoc Jones refused and consequently had to reconsider his denominational allegiance.[2] It was a great comfort to him that his father agreed with him, and this encouraged the son to continue his practice of visiting other churches apart from those of the Scotch Baptists. He decided to settle down in Mount Pleasant Baptist church under the ministry of J. H. Humphreys (1899-1911).[3]

Invitations to preach came regularly to Caradoc Jones. It was a great loss for the Scotch Baptists to lose such an effective preacher and it was a cause of grief to their descendants that the leaders of the day did not see the unusual potential of one of their own:[4]

I grieve to think that my own Fathers in the faith failed to discern this sixty years ago and had not utilised the young man in their midst to build up our churches. Never have we produced his like.

That was the opinion of T. W. Jones, M.P for Wrexham writing in 1962. He was right in saying that the Scotch Baptists leaders should have acted differently. They would not be agreeing with the settled, paid ministry by allowing Caradoc Jones to visit other denominations. Allowing him to visit them would have also helped to promote the discussion between the old Baptists and the Scotch Baptists. At that period, perhaps it was too much to expect such charity.

The promising preacher stood by his conviction, but it must have been a tremendous wrench for him to leave the denomination in which he had been nurtured. And, also, leaving meant disagreeing with some of his relatives. Several branches of the family could look back over a hundred years of honouring the Scotch Baptist tradition and some of them had worked with J. R. Jones, Ramoth. It must have been a burden for the relatives as well to disagree with one of their own family.

Mount Pleasant Baptist church was glad to have, not only another member, but also a promising preacher. The minister thought highly of Caradoc Jones. He had an opportunity to exercise his gifts in the chapel and in other places, especially in Chester Street Baptist church, Wrexham.[5] Caradoc Jones was still a committed Baptist but worshipping now with the old Baptists. There was a change linguistically, because Tabernacle was Welsh speaking, but Mount Pleasant was an English cause.

With such opportunities for ministry, Caradoc Jones thought seriously of preparing for the ministry of the word, full time. There were a number of possibilities as far as colleges were concerned. On one occasion he was preaching with the Primitive Methodists.[6] It was an afternoon service and the morning preacher from Manchester was present. He was so impressed with the preacher that he was invited to enter Manchester Wesleyan College. On another occasion a lecturer from the Baptist College at Bangor, north Wales, heard the preacher and, like the minister from Manchester, was deeply impressed.[7] The lecturer invited Caradoc Jones to enter the College at Bangor under a bursary scheme. J. H. Humphreys, the Mount Pleasant minister, had also mentioned the name of Caradoc Jones to the College at Bangor. He refused both offers but he did have something in mind concerning his preparation for future ministry.

ENTERING COLLEGE

Caradoc Jones' choice of a college was Spurgeon's College, London. There were many possible reasons for that choice although the preacher himself did not mention any. He had moved to an English speaking church that belonged to the Baptist Union of Great Britain. The name of C. H. Spurgeon was still revered in many parts of Wales. During the Downgrade Controversy he had a number of strong supporters in the country. Many people in Wales approved of his departure, on doctrinal grounds, from the Baptist Union. At the beginning of the twentieth century the minister at the Metropolitan Tabernacle, closely associated with the College, was Thomas Spurgeon, C. H. Spurgeon's son.[8] He was the President of the College. When he visited Wales during the Revival of 1904-5, he was welcomed as a pastor and as the son of his father.

Eleven other students were applying for admission to the College. When Caradoc Jones' turn came to be interviewed he was questioned regarding his preaching and the panel must have been surprised at the extent of his travel to preach. The President asked him if he had been preaching the previous Sunday. When Caradoc Jones answered in the affirmative the President asked him for a portion of the sermon:[9]

The young man rose to deliver his oration but was told to sit down. Although this was not his usual posture while preaching, he poured out the message that had first gripped his own soul before it was delivered to others, and doubtless his present congregation would have been given the entire sermon had not the President stopped the eager young preacher. Other applicants were awaiting their interviews, and time was passing. But he saw Dr McCaig, the Principal, pass a wink to Mr. Spurgeon which he interpreted as commendation, and later he confessed, 'I knew by that I was in the College'.

The other applicants were rather disturbed when Caradoc Jones told them on the way out that he had to preach before the panel. It is not known whether they were asked to give a sample of a sermon. If they were asked, it is doubtful if they delivered the message with the same eloquence as the preacher from Rhos.

A farewell meeting was held at Mount Pleasant 9 August 1903. The usual service took place when Caradoc Jones himself preached and at the close of the meeting a presentation was made to him. He received a 'Bible and dressing case' from Mount Pleasant and a 'handsome silk umbrella' from the members of the Primitive Methodists in Rhos. The minister, J. W. Humphreys, and others from Mount Pleasant spoke briefly and an earnest prayer was offered for the prospective student.[10]

Caradoc Jones had much experience as a preacher when he went Spurgeon's College in the autumn of 1903, but it was a traumatic experience for him to enter the College. He had received some education in the local school and had disciplined himself in reading books. Now, however, he was expected to learn new subjects in a strange environment far removed from the village life of Rhos. He was at home in the close knit community of that village but now he had to study regularly.

Dr McCaig, the Principal, was born near Perth, Scotland, in a

Presbyterian area. Immediately after his conversion at the age of sixteen, he began to preach, but he and some of his comrades were prosecuted for doing so. They were discharged because 'they were under a delusion that they were preaching the gospel'. [11] Convinced of Baptist principles, McCaig entered the Baptist ministry. He began as a tutor in the College in 1892 and became Principal in 1898. He took the whole of the College in theology. At the end of the year he reported that[12]

> In Theology we have been pursuing the old paths. In the Hodge class our topics have been the lofty ones of the Trinity, the divine Attributes, the divine Decrees and Predestination. Majesty and mystery have met us at every turn, but reverent faith in the word of Revelation has given firm foothold on the dizziest heights.

It was the Principal's conviction that Christology is the essence of Theology. Not since the Nicene Council, he declared, had there been such a need 'to have a clear conception of the New Testament Christology'.[13] He realized that the attack on the divine inspiration of Scripture had led to an attack on the Person of Christ. He was in the tradition of the founder of the College. McCaig loved Spurgeon and loved Spurgeon's gospel.

It is possible to think of Caradoc Jones having a 'firm foothold on the dizziest heights'. When it came to Latin, the Biblical languages and Butler's *Analogy*, he would be probably in the lowest depths. It was one of the problems of the College that it had no entrance examination and yet aimed at a classical education.[14]

Caradoc Jones was greatly helped by the fellowship of many of his fellow students, including an Australian and W. Forde from Barbados,[15] who, after the college days, went as a missionary to Costa Rica, under the auspices of the Jamaican Missionary Society. They also had difficulty in studying. One of the lecturers promised to give them extra tuition, but he was taken ill before he could fulfil his promise.[16] Another person who became a close friend of Caradoc Jones was William Fetler from Latvia.[17]

A number of Welshmen were in the College the same time as Caradoc Jones. Thomas Hayward from King Street, Blaenavon, had already entered in 1902. Others followed in 1903 and 1904. Austin Llewellyn Edwards was born in Haverfordwest. He was the son of Dr William Edwards, Principal of the Baptist College in that place and when it was moved to Cardiff. John R. Edwards, born in Thornton Heath, spent his boyhood in Trefgarn, Pembrokeshire, and was a nephew of Dr William Edwards. The student had ministered at Pen-y-darren, Merthyr, before entering the College. Frank Williams was from Pontnewydd and held a pastorate at Senghennydd, Caerphilly before starting on his course.[18] After leaving College, Christie Davies, from the Swansea Valley, spent twenty years with the Baptist Missionary Society in the Congo.[19]

Caradoc Jones valued the friendship of his fellow Welshmen, because they were from Wales, but also because some of them were gifted musically, something they had in common with Caradoc Jones. Some of the students were very close to him. Caradoc Jones used to take Forde and William Fetler to Rhos during the holiday period. [20] The Welshman was also glad of the company of Forde and the Australian as co-plodders in their studies. Some of his fellow students advised Caradoc Jones not to proceed to the second year because that was the most difficult of the whole course. Encouraged by the results of the first year, Caradoc Jones was determined to proceed and did so successfully.[21]

THE WELSH REVIVAL, 1904-5

By the beginning of his second year in College, revival had broken out in Wales. It originated in February 1903 when a young girl in Tabernacle, New Quay (Welsh Calvinistic Methodist), confessed that she loved the Lord Jesus Christ with all her heart. That meeting was transformed and the Holy Spirit gripped the congregation. The minister, Joseph Jenkins, had been concerned with the spiritual state of his denomination for many months and he himself had been led to a deeper experience of God. From February to September 1904 the fire spread to many parts in Ceredigion and to Newcastle Emlyn, over the border in Carmarthenshire.[22]

It was to Newcastle Emlyn that Evan Roberts and Sidney Evans went 13 September 1904 to prepare for the Christian ministry with the Welsh Calvinistic Methodists. During the same month, Seth Joshua of the Forward Movement of the Calvinistic Methodists arrived to take a mission in Newcastle Emlyn and New Quay. At a 7 o'clock meeting at Blaenannerch, Seth Joshua prayed the prayer, 'Bend us'. The words lodged in the heart of Evan Roberts. In the 9 o'clock meeting the words burned so fiercely that he had to pray 'Bend me, Bend me, Bend me, Oh! Oh! Oh!' The Spirit of God fell upon him and invaded the whole of his being. On 31 October 1904 he went home to Loughor near Swansea where he held meetings for a fortnight before moving to other parts of Wales.[23]

While Evan Roberts was holding meetings in Loughor, the Rev. R. B. Jones, Porth, was holding meetings in Rhos, the birthplace of Caradoc Jones. Meetings commenced on 8 November 1904 and continued until the 18th of the month.[24] The preacher hammered home the theme of the holiness of God. Many were humbled and some despaired as they realized their sinful condition in the sight of a holy God. Relief came when the good news of forgiveness in Christ was proclaimed. Congregations increased during the series of meetings, regular prayer meetings were held and processions through the streets were arranged, led very often by the Rhos Excelsior Band. Children of the Revival would gather together at an arranged spot, hold a meeting and then proceed along the streets, singing hymns. A characteristic of the processions in Rhos was the collections that were made for those in need.[25]

R. B. Jones returned to south Wales 19 November, but the Spirit continued to work powerfully in Rhos. Exceptionally high numbers of people were converted and sought membership in the churches. For example, at the beginning of December 1904, fifty-two applied for membership in the Welsh Calvinistic church and thirty received into membership at one of the Welsh Congregational churches.[26] All the denominations took part including the Anglican Church. Weekly reports appeared on the local paper, *Rhos Herald*, and the one responsible for them was the Scotch Baptist W. S. Jones, Caradoc Jones' brother.

It is evident from the reports that W. S. Jones was in wholehearted sympathy with the Revival. His, and Caradoc Jones' father and mother had related to them the story of the 1859 Revival and the Scotch Baptists were emphasizing the importance of experience as well as doctrine.[27] They were ready for revival. Tabernacle and Soar, the two Scotch Baptist churches, felt the influences of the Revival. A genuine work of God was taking place in the two places. Not many baptisms were recorded during the years immediately preceding the Revival but the Revival changed the situation: Tabernacle, 27 November 1904, 3; 11 December 1904, 11, 18 December 1904, 3. For a small church to receive seventeen members in less than a month was like a revolution. From November 1904 to the middle of January 1905, Tabernacle and Soar between them received 37 members and Mount Pleasant, to which Caradoc Jones belonged, received 40 into membership during the same period.[28]

Caradoc Jones must have been thrilled to receive accounts of the Revival from his brother, W. S. Jones, and others in Rhos and Ponciau. The minister of Mount Pleasant was prominent in the Revival and was a person that emphasized the material needs of the people as well as their spiritual needs. He would have liked to see some institution set up where the converts could meet socially and he also urged the children of the Revival to be active in society.[29]

Further information was received from the Rev. Thomas Phillips, Norwich. He had been to Wales early in December 1904 and had prayed for an opportunity to relate the story on his return to

England. The very first day after his arrival he received a telegram from Thomas Spurgeon, inviting him to a meeting in the Metropolitan Tabernacle.[30] In the meeting he introduced himself as one who had experienced the 1859 Revival and rejoiced that he was alive to experience another visitation of the Spirit of God. According to Thomas Phillips, three things were noticeable in the meetings: 1. That Evan Roberts is a man of prayer 2. That the results are not due to his preaching, for he speaks very little and always in the simplest fashion, and 3. That the power of the Holy Ghost is paramount. The pastor, who was on the verge of moving to Bloomsbury, believed that revival was England's greatest need, but that it could not be secured by copying Wales.[31]

CHRISTMAS 1904

With such information and hunger in his own soul, Caradoc Jones returned to Rhos for the Christmas holidays. The people of Rhos had a quiet week during the middle of December 1904, but the following week the Spirit of God moved mightily once again. Many were almost overcome with joy and praise. More than usual from surrounding districts were attending the meetings. When Caradoc Jones arrived he knew immediately that the village was in the grip of revival:[32]

> From the railway station he had a walk of over two miles through the dark streets, and as he approached the village he heard singing, the timbre of which seemed to be angelic. Although accustomed to good singing, having grown up in a district famed for its singers, the music held him as under a spell. Nearer and nearer it came until the beam of a miner's safety lamp pierced the darkness, to reveal a long procession of people singing on their way to the big chapel.

The 'big chapel' referred to was the Welsh Calvinistic chapel. Caradoc Jones had a hurried cup of tea, rushed to the meeting and arrived just before the procession that he had seen on the way. He had no doubt that the Spirit of God was at work.

For some reason his return to College was delayed and it gave him further opportunity to attend revival meetings. He sent a report of some of the events to Spurgeon's College. [33] He traced the background to the Revival, especially the visit of Rosina Davies, the evangelist, and the revival meetings in Ponciau during June and July 1904. After summarizing the visit of R. B. Jones in November, Caradoc Jones proceeded to mention some meetings and some of the characteristics of the Revival. During Christmas and New Year's Day all the chapels were full with all classes of people. The singing was always good in Rhos but now it had 'Revival Soul in it'.[34] Most of the hymns were Welsh ones, but there were a few favourite English hymns: 'The Lamb, the Lamb, the bleeding Lamb' and 'I need Thee every hour' and the 'Oh' would 'swell like a wave of supplication'.

One of the most popular Welsh hymns was based on the meeting between Jesus Christ and the woman of Samaria. The Rev. Howell Elvet Lewis (Elfed), well-known minister and hymn writer, introduced it to the people of Rhos. Caradoc Jones included a translation in his letter:[35]

> Christ once on Jacob's fountain,
> Did rest him on the way.
> He travelled through Samaria,
> Oh travel here today.
> He thirsted there while resting,
> To save the sinful men.
> And still he's thirsting, thirsting,
> For saving more again.

Refrain: More, more, for saving more again,
> And still he's thirsting, thirsting
> For saving more again.

The words and the tune appealed to the congregation. The hymn was based on a well-known story in Scripture and concentrated on conversion. The tune gave plenty of opportunity to repeat, especially the 'More, more'. Both together, the words and the tune, formed an appeal to the sinner to return to the Saviour.

Often, there was a moving moment in a meeting when separated parties were reconciled. Caradoc Jones refers to a meeting when a person got up, walked to the front and confessed that he was not at peace with his brother. Almost immediately that brother got up, walked to the front, confessing his sin. Both of them embraced in the big seat. The student was also impressed with the processions. Some would run away when the procession was passing, afraid to be influenced by the children of Revival, while others joined and many of them would be converted. Caradoc Jones commented on the preaching:[36]

> As to the preaching, I will only say that all the sermons find their way to Calvary. The discourses are a little shorter than usual, and are very pointed; we seem to take kindlier to arrows than we have ever done before.

Preaching had an important place in the Revival in Rhos.

VISITS TO WALES
Some of the Welsh students arrived back at the College before Caradoc Jones returned. They were full of what they had seen and experienced during the vacation in south Wales. For example, Christie Davies had taken part in Revival meetings in the Swansea Valley, including a service underground with the colliers. He had joined in with them in their intense singing and praying.[37] Another student that visited revival meetings in south and north Wales was William Fetler, one of Caradoc Jones' friends. The Latvian visited Ruabon where he stayed with Morgan Jones and his wife. During his

stay, William Fetler, as was his custom, spoke very personally to his hosts. He challenged them concerning their commitment to Christ. They acknowledged that it was not what it should be. The three bowed in prayer and committed themselves anew to the Saviour. Early next morning William Fetler could be heard singing 'I surrender all to Thee, my Blessed Saviour'. Morgan Jones and his wife went upstairs and joined him in the singing.[38]

William Fetler visited Cardiff and the Rhondda. When he took part in a meeting in Tabernacle, Cardiff, the minister, Charles Davies, marvelled at the freedom the student had in prayer. There was a remarkable power in Fetler's praying and preaching. The Revival influenced him deeply, and a meeting with Evan Roberts strengthened his desire to see revival in Latvia and Russia.[39]

The Metropolitan Tabernacle and the College were not only aware of what was happening in Wales, they felt as if they were part of the Revival. The Welshmen there continued to receive reports from home. Caradoc Jones, Christie Davies and William Fetler had returned with vivid descriptions of Revival events. Representatives from the Tabernacle and the College decided to visit as well. Dr McCaig gave his report in the prayer meeting 16 January 1905.[40] He gave his impression of Evan Roberts. According to the Principal, the revivalist was of a 'Highly-strung nature', but his emotions were under the control of the Holy Spirit. His emphasis was on worship and believing. He would remind the congregation that they were in the presence of God and, whatever was sung, would ask 'Do you believe it?' His favourite theme in his addresses was the death of Christ on Calvary.[41]

Describing the meetings that he attended, Dr McCaig drew attention to their intensity, intense prayer, intense singing and intense joy. He was also struck by the variety of the meetings. They were not stereotyped. There was much singing and praying in all meetings. In one meeting singing would be predominant, in another meeting, prayer. Sometimes preaching had an important place in a service, while at other times there would be very little preaching, only a few short addresses. The intensity of feeling varied in degree, sometimes it was humbling, so humbling that many were a long time before coming to faith. At other times the conviction of sin was lighter and not so profound. Joy could be something deep in the heart, at other time finding expression in praise. In one of the meetings, Christie Davies the student was present. It was his singing of the well-known 'Pen Calfaria', that restored self-control when Evan Roberts broke down with emotion.[42]

Dr McCaig and Thomas Spurgeon went back the second time to Wales. A person from the English Baptist church in Bridgend had written to Thomas Spurgeon, informing him of the conversion of a deacon, a figure well known in the town and in the county.[43] The visitors attended meetings in Bridgend, Merthyr and Pontypridd. At Bridgend and Pen-y-darren, Merthyr, Thomas Spurgeon was asked to speak because he was of the Spurgeon family. In Merthyr they also heard Evan Roberts once again. That particular meeting started sometime before the arrival of the revivalist. The congregation sang and prayed. Evan Roberts and the two Misses Davies entered as the congregation was singing 'Diolch Iddo' (Praise Him) and 'Pen Calfaria'. Singing, praying and giving testimonies continued, with 'occasional words of wisdom and tenderness from Mr Roberts'.[44] What seemed to be the last hymn was announced, but many in the congregation started to sing and pray again. Evan Roberts spoke on the suffering of Christ on the Cross and the congregation sang 'All hail the power of Jesus name' and one of Evan Roberts' favourites, 'Who is a pardoning God like Thee?'[45]

During the visit, the visitors met the Rev. O. M. Owen, Pen-y-darren, Merthyr Tydfil, who shared his experiences with them. At Pontypridd they met Awstin, Revival correspondent of the *Western Mail* and it was in Pontypridd that they attended an underground meeting in a colliery. The singing and the prayers were fervent and Thomas Spurgeon was invited to say a word. He made use of a hymn that they had sung, 'Lead, kindly light amidst the encircling gloom', and addressed the colliers:[46]

'Now, you all have lamps, will each man hold up his lamp to his face and I'll hold mine up and then we shall be able to see each other better'. This was done, and it was a memorable sight to see these begrimed faces shining in the light of the lamps, and not a few of them manifestly shining with the glory of the greater Light. 'Now' said Mr. Spurgeon, 'we can look each other in the face'. 'Ah', he added, 'and thank God, we can look Him in the face if we are trusting Jesus'.

The Londoners had no doubt that the Revival was 'the Lord's doing and marvellous in our eyes'.[47]

TABERNACLE AND COLLEGE MEETINGS
These visits to Wales and the return of the students after the Christmas vacation had a marked influence on the Tabernacle and the College. They received further information from the daily and weekly papers. They were well informed concerning the Revival and many of them had personal experience of the meetings. Consequently the thinking of College and chapel concerning revival was molded by the Revival in Wales. Both places made urgent appeals for prayer and the burden of that praying was for revival. After six weeks of prayer, the Tabernacle members and the students in the College were moved to hold a series of meetings with the main aim to reach the outsiders. They arranged the meetings from the 13 March to the beginning of April 1905.[48] The Welsh students were asked to lead: 'The happy thought was suggested to the Pastor that the six Welsh students at the college, who had all, during the Christmas vacation, been in close touch with the Revival movement in their homes and were full of its spirit, should be invited to conduct the Mission, it being felt that the the very fact of their Welsh nationality would appeal to outsiders'.[49]

The first meeting was held in the Lecture Hall but they had to move to the chapel the second night and after a few meetings the first gallery had to be opened. The singing was lively and the prayers intense, so much like the revival meetings in Wales. Apart from the congregational singing, some of the students, including the Welshmen and a Scotsman, sang solos and addressed the meetings. In some of the meetings, as many as fifty and sixty responded to the call of the gospel.[50]

Processions were arranged at different times of the day, but a characteristic of the witness was the midnight processions. They aimed at bringing those on the street to the Tabernacle. Dr McCaig describes how 'The friends mustered outside the Tabernacle at 11 o'clock, and, marshalled by the students with bannered bills announcing the meetings and a few cornet players leading the singing, a goodly procession was formed'.[51] The procession continued on its way[52]

> Down St George's Road, round by Christ Church, in front of which a halt was made and a special invitation given to wayfarers to attend the meeting, on to the Canterbury Music Hall in Westminster Road, then across the 'New Cut', up Waterloo Road and back by London Road to the 'Elephant and Castle', and so back to the Tabernacle, the procession wended its way creating no small stir among the denizens of the district and the people in the streets.

The meeting went on until 3 o'clock in the morning. A similar account of a procession was reported from Pontycymer, Wales, with one difference. Some of those in their drink brought their dogs with them.[53]

The students, including Caradoc Jones, took a prominent part in these revival meetings. They addressed the congregations; sang solos and formed a quartette. Members of the quartette were Caradoc Jones, Christy Davies, Jack Edwards and Austin Edwards.[54]

Although, as in Wales, much time was given to singing, the students and others would always preach. Examples of texts chosen by the students were: 'Whatever a man soweth, that shall he also reap'; 'What think ye of Christ?' or a topic, 'Opening the Books', 'solemn and impressive'.[55]

They also had an opportunity to do personal work. Caradoc Jones was a very wise soul winner. During a meeting in the Elephant and Castle, a number of midnight meetings were held for those that were willing to come off the streets. These were held even when no procession preceded them. One evening two girls came in together. They were in a frivolous mood and one of them left immediately at the end of the meeting, but the other one stayed in her seat. As Caradoc Jones passed her, she turned to him, and said: 'I am going to the devil'. He replied: 'You are too good for the devil and not too bad for Jesus Christ. He can save you'. She left hurriedly.[56]

Sometime later, Caradoc Jones received a letter from her, telling him how her mother had been praying for her. She signed the letter 'A broken reed'. Caradoc Jones showed the letter to Dr McCaig who passed it on to Thomas Spurgeon. The Welshman was anxious that others knew of the girl in case he would be criticized for communicating with a girl from off the streets. Caradoc Jones received further letters from her, pleading for a meeting with him. After some consideration, he agreed to meet her in Hyde Park:[57]

> She behaved correctly, and offered him a parcel. When he said he could not accept it, she threw it away, saying that a man had given her a sovereign, which was not the price of prostitution, and with it she had brought Mr. Jones two books. He picked up the package and opened it. One of the books was a volume of George Herbert's poetry.

Caradoc Jones was not sure of what had been achieved through that meeting, but had the satisfaction that he had met her and had tried to help her.

The girl attended another meeting in the Elephant and Castle. Caradoc Jones and another student were to speak that evening. He thought it wise to preach first and then leave the meeting. Someone else could deal with the girl at the close of the service. He later found out that she was converted that evening. She dedicated her life to the Saviour, and later became the Matron in a Home for needy girls, many of whom were prostitutes.[58]

In the last meeting of the series there wasn't the usual spontaneous response. Caradoc Jones got up and read the letter he had received from the girl who had signed herself as 'A broken read'. A strong emotion moved the congregation to praise God. They were reminded of the saving grace of God. Another appeal was made and there was much response to the call of the gospel.[59] As in revival meetings in Wales, the appeal was made in the meetings at the Elephant and Castle.

The series of meetings during March and April were followed by a Thanksgiving service on the 7 May[60] and a Conference on 'Revival' on the 18 of the same month.[61] In the Thanksgiving Service, Thomas Spurgeon preached on Col 2: 6, 'As ye have therefore received Christ Jesus the Lord, so walk ye in Him'. In the conference the Welsh quartette took part and the Rev. O. M. Owen, Pen-y-darren, Merthyr, shared his experiences of the Revival in Wales.[62] The guest speaker was Dr Saillens of Paris. He also had visited Wales during the Revival when he attended meetings in Cardiff, Nant-y-moel and other places.[63] He was friendly with C. H. Spurgeon and had corresponded with Thomas Spurgeon for a number of years, but they met personally during 1900. Both Dr Saillens and Thomas Spurgeon were staunch Baptists, concerned with revival and mission. Both supported the Pioneer Mission, a Baptist Mission dedicated to pioneering work and support weak churches. The church where Dr Saillens ministered, and his son in law after him, was to play an important part in the future life of Caradoc Jones.

In his address at the Conference, Dr Saillens described revival as a manifestation of the glory of God to the Church and to the world at large. Such a manifestation is accomplished by the Holy Spirit. The source is God himself and no human effort can produce a revival. All present would agree with Dr Saillens. In the last meeting the Welsh quartette sang the English words 'We'll view from the mountains of Canaan' to the tune 'Crugybar'.[64]

Other meetings were held. The Fourth Auxiliary of the Work in France took place, in which Dr Saillens spoke and in which the Welsh Quartette took part.[65] A midnight meeting was arranged for 25 August that was part of the preparation for a brief Mission in September.[66] It followed the same pattern as that of the earlier one, the students once again taking the lead. The meetings were spontaneous and the students preached on evangelistic texts, having the outsider in mind. This is evident from such texts as Luke 18, the Parable of the Pharisee and the Publican, 'In the Name of Jesus of Nazareth, rise up and walk', and John 3:3, the new birth.[67]

TIME TO LEAVE

Caradoc Jones completed his college course and was due to leave in 1907, the same time as William Fetler. The Pioneer Mission had persuaded Fetler to return to Russia because he had been in two minds concerning his future. He felt drawn to his own people but also believed that God could call him to China. When Fetler was ready to leave for Russia, Caradoc Jones accompanied him to the East London Docks:[68]

While I waited on the quay-wall (from 8 p.m. until midnight!) he went on board to speak to the crew of the Christ that could quell the raging sea. At midnight the bell rang for their departure. Fetler waved to me and asked me to sing one of our beautiful Welsh hymns. A lump rose in my throat at seeing this brave one leave among the ungodly crew. I shook my head but he called out 'Do sing to encourage me'. There was nothing for it but obey, so I sang the hymn which we sing to 'Crugybar'.

We'll view from the mountains of Canaan
Our paths through the wilderness here:
And, then, all the steps of the journey
In Heaven's perfect light will be clear.
We'll think of the tempests and terrors,
Of death and the grave now all oe'r,
And we from all harm ever resting
In God's perfect peace evermore.

It is possible that Caradoc Jones was the translator. It is known that he translated hymns, and this particular translation is not found in the hymn collections of the Revival in Wales. The translation generally is quite successful. The main weakness is the last line, because it fails to capture the idea of 'swimming in God's love' found in the original. The time came for Caradoc Jones to leave. He received a call from two small churches in Cardiff. He was also concerned about the witness of the gospel in Brittany; a concern that was formed during his college days. When he went to Cardiff, he made it clear that if he received a call to Brittany he would leave as soon as possible.[69]

The College period had been formative for Caradoc Jones. He was better trained for the ministry, more convinced of Baptist principles and had experienced a time of revival. In London he came in contact with leading Baptists like Dr McCaig, Thomas Spurgeon, Dr Saillens, of the church at the rue Meslay in Paris, and his son-in-law Arthur Blocher, who, like his father-in-law supported the Pioneer Mission. The student had matured much before entering College through the influence of home, church, work and the experience of preaching regularly. The foundation was there and during his College days Caradoc Jones made sure that it was a foundation on which he could build. When he left the College he was thirty-two years old and some students that had left had spent a number of years in the ministry at that age. There is no doubt that he had been well prepared to start on his first ministry in Cardiff, that had just been made a city in 1905.

1 'Rhosllannerchrugog, Cyfarfodydd Diwygiadol', *Yr Ymwelydd*, April 1901.
2. *Knight in Royal Service*, 10.
3. Myrddin Davies, 'Cyfnodau a Digwyddiadau', *Bedyddwyr Rhosllannerch-- rugog*. The people of Mount Pleasant had met in Soar for a brief period, before their chapel was built: *Trafodion Cymdeithas Hanes y Bedyddwyr*, 1940, 65.
4. Angus Library, Oxford, Pioneer Mission Collection: Scrap Book, article taken from the *Rhos Herald*, 10 November 1962.
5. According to Mrs Edna Evans, né Jones, Ponciau, Caradoc Jones' niece.
6. *Knight in Royal Service*, 10.
7. Ibid.
8. Thomas Spurgeon, W. H. Fullerton, *Thomas Spurgeon* (London, 1919); Eric Hayden, *The Spurgeon Family* (Pilgrim Publications, Pasadena, 1993), ch. 9.
9. *Knight in Royal Service*, 11.
10. 'Rhos', *Rhos Herald*, 15 August 1903.
11. Mike Nicholls, *Lights of the World* (Nu print, Harpenden, 1994), 127-8.
12. 'Annual Paper Concerning the work in connection with the Pastor's College', included in *The Sword and the Trowel*, 1905.
13. Ibid.
14. Nicholls , *Lights of the World*, 108.
15. 'Notes', *The Sword and the Trowel*, September 1907
16. *Knight in Royal Service*, 12.
17. Noel Gibbard, *On the Wings of the Dove* (Bryntirion Press, 2002), chap. 1:5.
18. Information regarding students kindly received from Spurgeon's College.
19. J. W. Hughes, *A Brief Memoir* (London, 1962); T. M. Bassett, *The Baptists of Wales and the BMS* (Swansea, 1991), 66-7.
20. According to Mrs Edna Evans, né Jones, Ponciau.
21. *Knight in Royal Service*, 12.
22. Background, Eifion Evans, *The Welsh Revival of 1904* (Evangelical Movement of Wales, Port Talbot, 1969).
23. Ibid.
24. W. S. Jones, *Y Diwygiad yn Rhosllanerchrugog (sic)* (from the *Rhos Herald*, 25 June 1904 to 21 January 1905), 4-6.
25. Noel Gibbard, *Caniadau'r Diwygiad* (Bryntirion Press, 2003), 71.
26. W. S. Jones, *Y Diwygiad yn Rhosllanerchrugog*, (sic), 32
27. *Knight in Royal Service*, 12.
28. 'Tabernacl a Soar, Rhos', *Yr Ymwelydd*, January-February 1905; W. S. Jones, *Y Diwygiad yn Rhosllanerchrugog* (sic), 32.

29. 'Gohebiaeth', *Rhos Herald*, 2 March 1905; idem. 'Cymanfa Ddirwestol Dwyreinbarth Dinbych', 28 October 1905.
30. 'Times of refreshing', *The Sword and the Trowel*, January 1905.
31. Ibid.
32. *Knight in Royal Service*, 13-4.
33. 'What God hath Wrought', *The Sword and the Trowel*, February 1905.
34. Ibid.
35. Ibid.
36. Ibid.
37. *On the Wings of the Dove*, 215.
38. 'Editorial', *Riches of Grace*, September 1935, and including summary of Fetler's address at the Apostolic Convention of that year.
39. *On the Wings of the Dove*, 215.
40. 'What God hath Wrought', *The Sword and the Trowel*, February 1905.
41. Ibid.
42. Ibid.
43. Ibid., 'With Pastor Thomas Spurgeon in the Welsh Revival', March 1905.
44. Ibid.
45. Ibid.
46. Ibid.
47. Ibid.
48. Ibid. 'The Revival at the Tabernacle Continued', April 1905.
49. Ibid.
50. Ibid.
51. Ibid.
52. Ibid.
53. Noel Gibbard, *Caniadau'r Diwygiad* , 73.
54. *Knight in Royal Service*, 14.
55. 'The Revival at the Tabernacle continued', *The Sword and the Trowel*, May 1905.
56. *Knight in Royal Service*, 15.
57. Ibid. 15-6.
58. Ibid.
59. Ibid.
60. 'A Thanksgiving Communion Service at the Tabernacle', *The Sword and the Trowel*, June 1905.
61. Ibid. 'The College Conference'.
62. Ibid.
63. *On the Wings of the Dove*, 24-5.
64. 'Notes on Revivals', *The Sword and the Trowel*, August 1905.
65. Ibid., 'Pasteur Saillen's Annual Meeting', November 1905.
66. Ibid., 'An Account of a short mission at the Tabernacle', October 1905.
67. Ibid.
68. Caradoc Jones, 'The 1904-5 Revival', *The Evangelical Magazine of Wales*, November 1968.
69. *Knight in Royal Service*, 19.

The Jones family.
From left to right, back row: Caradoc, Frederick, Henry, William (father),
William S., Mariah (mother), David
(Photograph presented by Mrs Beryl Hall, Cardiff)

Herber House, Pontfadog
The house was built in 1851; used in turn by Methodists and Scotch Baptists
(*100 Years in the Valley*, 1999, p.122)

Soar Scotch Baptist, Ponciau
(By permission of Mr Arfon Pritchard, Rhos, and the National Library, Aberystwyth)

Tabernacle Scotch Baptist
(By permission of Mr Arfon Pritchard, Rhos, and the National Library, Aberystwyth)

Mount Pleasant English Baptist
(By permission of Mr Arfon Pritchard, Rhos, and the National Library, Aberystwyth)

The Welsh Students at Spurgeon's College, London.
Standing, from left to right: Christie Davies, Jack Edwards, Caradoc Jones and
Austin Edwards (the Quartette).
Seated: Frank Williams and Thomas Hayward. (From *Knight in Royal Service*, p.14)

Garden Party at 'Bronwydd', Pen-y-lan, Cardiff, 1925.
From left to right: Rev. Caradoc Jones, Rev. E. A. Carter (Pioneer Mission),
Mr Evan Nicholas, Tabernacle, Cardiff, Mrs Morgan Davies, Cardiff, who opened
the function, and her husband, Morgan Davies; they were also members of
Tabernacle. (From the *Pioneer Review*, July-September, 1925)

Pastor Caradoc Jones and the deacons of Gabalfa English Baptist Church, 1913
(By permission of the pastor of the church)

Co-workers.
From left to right:
A. Huck,
Caradoc Jones
and
Arthur Matthews.
(From Magazine
Eglise Réformée,
July 1991, p.10.
Copy kindly sent by
the Rev. Michael
McGowan)

The new chapel, 1930 (From *Knight in Royal Service*, p.30)

Caradoc Jones and the orphans, 1933
(Magazine *Eglise Reformée*, p.10. Copy kindly sent by the Rev. Michael McGowan)

Church group, 1933

(Magazine *Eglise Réformée*, p.25. Copy kindly sent by the Rev. Michael McGowan)

Madame
Masclet and
three orphans.

(From *The
Pioneer Review*,
January-March,
1939)

The tablecloth made in the
Internment Camp, Vittel, and
presented to Caradoc Jones.
Arrived in Tabernacle Welsh
Baptist church via Sylvia Le
Saux, Havard Gregory and
Beryl Hall.

(Photograph, Mrs Leah Millinship,
Cardiff)

The Orphanage, 'Revenez-Y', 1947. (From *Knight in Royal Service*, p. 33)

Caradoc Jones visiting the gypsies. (From *Knight in Royal Service*, p.46)

The grave of Arthur Matthews at Kerity, Brittany.
(Photograph, Michel Garsmeur, Paimpol)

Caradoc Jones and Nurse Thompson outside 'Llydaw', New Street, Rhos,
after returning to Rhos in 1967.
(Photograph sent by Michael McGowan. Copy made by Mrs Leah Millinship, Cardiff)

Caradoc Jones at 80.
(From *Knight in Royal Service*, p6)

3

LENGTHENING THE CORDS AND
STRENGTHENING THE STAKES: CARDIFF
1907-20

Many friends parted as they left College during 1906-7. Thomas
Hayward left for Lewin Road, Streatham; Christie Davies for Africa;
William Fetler for Russia, W. Forde to Costa Rica and Caradoc Jones
for Cardiff.[1] It is a reminder of the tremendous influence that a
theological college can wield in many parts of the world.

CARDIFF
Peter Finch, in his enthralling account of journeys in Cardiff, refers
to the immediate past of the city: 'There was a time, one which many
who live here now can remember, when the place stank permanently
of coal, fume and ash'.[2] The industrial development is reflected in
the growth of population. In 1901 it was 128,000, seven times what it
was in 1851.[3] The great influx by a vast number of very different
people transformed the whole life of Cardiff. The Docks had been
developed from 1839, but with the increase in the production of coal
in many areas, especially in Merthyr, Dowlais and the Rhondda, the
Docks flourished. Only 125 ship owners were listed for Cardiff in
1875, but by 1905 the number had risen to 256.[4] By that time Cardiff
was one of the biggest coal exporters in the world. The city (city from
1905) became cosmopolitan with Welsh, English, Greeks,
Norwegians and Dutch living together. More people were found on
the streets, and Bute Street had the reputation of being a rough area.

More children were found on the streets, creating their own culture with their games and rhymes.

Business was thriving and many businessmen moved out from the centre to other areas. New districts were being created, very different from each other. The Parade would be very different from Bute Street. A number of those described as 'gentlemen' lived in the Parade as well as a few Nonconformist ministers. Other areas to the north were developed and Cathays, Maindy and Gabalfa had their particular works. The Taff Vale Railway Company had its works in Cathays. Blackweir and Maindy had their Patent Fuel works and Gabalfa its Soap Works. By 1875, Cathays was a suburb of Cardiff and by 1900 the urbanisation was virtually completed. Only two working farms were left in the area. Gabalfa took a little longer to change, but 'By the outbreak of World War One, the open fields of Gabalfa were already disappearing and the land as far north as the modern interchange was brought into Cardiff's boundaries'.[5]

THE CHURCHES AND A CHANGING SOCIETY

It was not only the industrialists that were interested in the growth of Cardiff. The churches realized that they had to adapt to continual changes. More churches were being built. While there were only 46 churches in 1882, the number had increased to 114 by 1906.[6] The Welsh language churches were conscious of change. Some of them had been strengthened by the influx of Welsh speakers from other parts of Wales, many of them working as servants in large houses in the city. Surprisingly, perhaps, Cardiff had 329 monoglot Welshmen in 1906.[7] Welsh chapels grasped the opportunity to establish causes in developing areas. For example, Ebeneser Welsh Congregational church and Pembroke Place Welsh Presbyterian church started new causes in Cathays.[8]

On the other hand, the Welsh churches knew that the influx of people would lead to Anglicization. Canton Baptist church was English, but 'formerly Welsh' and the same description is given of

Clifton Calvinistic Methodist.[9] The majority of churches worked through the medium of English, and their ranks were strengthened with the emergence of the Forward Movement of the Presbyterian Church of Wales with its aim of reaching those outside the Church.[10] There is no doubt that it was much easier for the English churches to make progress than the Welsh churches.

TREDEGARVILLE BAPTIST CHURCH

One of the most missionary-minded churches in Cardiff was Tredegarville English Baptist church on the Parade.[11] It had only been established in 1861 in a room above a stable, but in a very short time the church was active in many places in Cardiff. Down in the Docks it supported the work of the John Cory Sailors' Rest in Bute Street. The Cory brothers were ship owners, coal exporters and liberal philanthropists. Richard Cory was the most liberal benefactor of Tredegarville and Longcross Street, while John Cory was one of the main supporters of Roath Wesleyan church.[12] Both of them contributed regularly to religious and philanthropic causes. One of the most zealous workers in Tredegarville was Harriet Tilley, daughter of a former pastor, who died in Cardiff in 1905. She married Pastor Cadot, France, who was much influenced by the Welsh Revival of 1904-5.[13] Alfred Tilley was a true pioneer. It was said of him that 'The founding of Village Stations and Mission Churches was characteristic of Mr. Tilley and became characteristic of the Church'.[14] He was also the prime mover in establishing a Missionary Society for Africa to follow the work of David Livingstone.[15]

The Tredegarville church spread its wing over Rumney to the east and Llanishen to the north. The church was interested in two other areas, Maindy-Gabalfa and Cathays.[16] The first meetings in Maindy-Gabalfa were held in a cottage, situated between the present Blackweir public house and the Gabalfa Junction. Along that stretch of road a number of works were located, including the Patent Fuel

Works and the Soap Works. The place of meeting belonged to the Patent Fuel Works. An entry for 20 October 1880 recorded that 'Our brother Criddle gave a very interesting account of the work being carried on by Brother Willis and himself at Blackweir'.[17] When the cottage was condemned, the worshippers moved to Cross Street, opposite the present church. A service was held on the plot of ground bought for building, 12 November 1883 and the new church was opened in 1884.[18] Local preachers were responsible for the work apart for one brief period when the branch church had a full time minister.

Two years later, in 1882, there was another reference to the activity of brother Willis. A report stated that 'Brother Willis had commenced a meeting at Cathays which is very encouraging'.[19] This was at Thesiger Street where the Sunday school was flourishing with fifty attending, cared for by four teachers. The next move was to Merthyr Street and then to Cathays Terrace. Soon after moving to Cathays Terrace there was need for a new building. That building was found in Pentyrch Street and was opened in 1905.[20]

Members in both Maindy and Pentyrch Street enjoyed the same privileges as the mother church in Tredegarville:[21] 'Any person wishing to join at either station must be received at that station first, and his name sent to the parent church, which appoints two visitors, one person from the station which he is wishful to join and the other from the parent church'.

The stations were self-supporting and paid for all expenses including pulpit supplies. The Revival of 1904-5 had a marked influence on Tredegarville: 'Tredegarville was filled to capacity Sunday after Sunday and its Mission Stations were providing spheres of service for the young people'.[22] The Revival was the main reason for the increase in membership. By the end of 1905, the church was in a very strong position:[23]

	Sittings				
	Chapel	School Room	Deacons Elders	Communi cants	Adherents
Tredegarville	1,000	700	12	833	450
Pentyrch St.	300	140	8	102	180
Maindy	300	50	6	65	90

There are three main aspects to these details. The number of communicants in Tredegarville is very high. Another aspect is the high number of leaders in Pentyrch and Maindy, but the most striking one is the remarkably high number of adherents in all three places. In Tredegarville the number was over half of that of the communicants. The adherents were those who attended but had not been received into membership. They could be quite high in a rural area but more so in an industrial area.

ASSISTANT PASTOR AND PASTOR

Growing, bustling Cardiff had two visitors in 1907. One of them was on a brief visit but the other one did not know how long he was going to stay. King Edward, who had granted city status in 1905, had a royal welcome. A day's holiday was announced to celebrate that special occasion. The other person was Caradoc Jones who had come to minister in Maindy and Cathays. He did not have a spectacular reception, but he knew that he was serving the King of kings. The preacher did not come for a holiday, but to call the believers of Cardiff to wage war against the enemies of God.

Caradoc Jones settled down and had a home with Mrs Richards in 8 Brithdir Street. As assistant pastor, until 1911, he was paid £120 a year. Maindy contributed £48-11-6, probably part of the £120.[24] Even for an assistant pastor this was not a very high wage, but he was single, and, therefore, it was sufficient. It is not known that 'he often gave back a good part of his cheque'.[25]

Two local congregations had been established, one in Maindy and the other in Cathays The majority of the members of both places lived very near to the church, and many of them had come from the west of England. It is possible to identify some west country families in the Maindy membership register: the Criddle, Watts and Lansdowne families were from Somerset; the Fenton and Ursell families from Gloucester, and the Dimond family came from Devon. There were only two Davieses and just one Jones.[26] Members of the families mentioned, followed different occupations, such as: 'Labourer Fuel Works'; 'Dock Labourer'; 'Railway Labourer', all related to the industrial development of Cardiff. Not all the occupations are given, but there was at least one 'Dressmaker'; one of the Criddle family was a 'General Dealer Rags & bones Coal & Furniture', and one of his sons was a 'Clerk in the book Trade'[27]

Many of the families were related. This was true of the Criddles, Lansdownes and Phillips families. Many in the same family and those related to them, lived in the same street. Seventeen members lived in Cross Street, of whom ten were of the Criddle family, four of the Carder family and two of the Lansdowne family. Other families in the street were from Cardiff itself, Scotland and Newcastle.[28] Maindy was an English church in a developing English area. This was an aspect of the general position in Cardiff. Caradoc Jones, a Welsh speaking Welshman from north Wales, settled in Maindy English Baptist church. He had already had much experience in preaching in English before going to Spurgeon's College and during his stay in the College. As a person from Rhos, he would be familiar with industrial development.

The new pastor was aware of the demands upon him and the possible opposition to the work. Early pioneers had been bitterly attacked. It was so bad on occasions that guards were appointed to warn of coming danger. Even when the open-air witnesses were not attacked, they were pelted and ridiculed. Caradoc Jones, knowing of possible danger, was not deterred: [29]

The Lord honoured the courage of his young servant by providing him with an aide in the person of a respected blind member of the fellowship who volunteered to accompany him wherever he went in that area, and not once was he molested.

Caradoc Jones felt that he had to venture outside of the church. The fire of the 1904-5 Revival was still burning in his heart and nothing could prevent him from 'throwing out the life line' to those without Christ. By this time he had also been to College. Spirit and mind had been prepared for ministry.

EARLY PROGRESS

Not only did Caradoc Jones have a guide at his side, he also had the good hand of God upon him. Tokens of blessing were evident soon after his arrival in Cardiff. Many were converted and some of the converts were from outside the church: [30]

> A large proportion of the men of the district were employed at the Patent Fuel works, and on New Year's Eve many who formerly squandered their wages in drink were to be seen at the Watch Night service, their begrimed faces and clothes indicating that they had come straight off the shift.

The fruit of the gospel was being made known, not only in church but in the home and in work as well.

A drop in membership had happened by the end of 1906, but this early fruit of the ministry increased the numbers. Pastor and people were grateful to God for confirming the call to Cardiff. The pastor himself was able to report at the end of his second year of ministry:[31]

> We have had a few losses through lapses and letters, especially in Pentyrch Street; but we have to praise God for the constant tokens of His favours to both Churches. We have been gladdened by the numbers that have come forward for baptism, thereby leaving us at the close of the year with a considerable increase in membership. We give God thanks, and take courage.

The increase is revealed in the statistics of the churches:[32]

1907:

Cathays	107	Total for Tredegarville and four stations
Maindy	52	1,079

1909:

Cathays	120	Total Tredegarville and four stations
Maindy	96	1,056

Tredegarville had spread her wings widely and was brooding over a thousand Baptists in Cardiff. It was the strongest Nonconformist church in the city and could have concentrated on building an empire, but instead the church decided to serve others. It is true that there was a denominational motive behind the evangelism, but the main inspiration was the gospel itself. Men, women and children had to be brought into a saving knowledge of the Lord Jesus Christ.

Llanishen, one of the Tredegarville branches, became independent in 1911. During the same time, Maindy and Cathays were considering uniting in order to form one pastorate. Discussions went ahead but it was decided to remain separate and for each church to have its own pastor.[33] During that same year, 1911, Caradoc Jones attended the World Baptist Alliance in America. He could have stayed there, because he was invited to be pastor of a Welsh Baptist church in Scranton. Caradoc Jones, however, was convinced that his place was in Cardiff. God had led him there and progress was being made. He could not stay in America. When he returned, both Maindy and Cathays invited him to be their pastor and, typical of Caradoc Jones, he chose Maindy, where he would face a tougher task than in Cathays.[34]

A NEW BUILDING

Caradoc Jones was now a pastor of one church. It was possible for him to concentrate on a smaller district, but there was a need for a new building that would hold more people and be a place of influence in the area. A committee was formed and a building scheme was launched. The building was in progress during 1912 and one way to raise support for the new venture was to hold a Bazaar. Writing an appeal on behalf of the church, Caradoc Jones introduced it by quoting Isaiah 54, verse 2: 'Enlarge the place of they tent, and let them stretch forth the curtains of thine habitation: spare not, lengthen they cords, and strengthen thy stakes'. [35] William Carey, the plodder, found comfort in those words, but he had to persevere for a long time before he saw visible fruit. Caradoc Jones was speaking of enlarging the tent because the present one was too small. He was expecting the people to flock to the meetings. He also knew that they would have to strengthen the stakes.

The project was an ambitious one. It included a chapel to seat 700, schoolrooms and a caretaker's house. The building was of Welsh stone, costing £4,000, which was a large sum in those days.[36] It took the church a number of years to clear the debt. A feature of the interior was the baptistry in front of the pulpit, placed there at the request of the pastor. The pastor's dream had been realized and he felt that he could lead his people on to greater things.

The chapel, Gabalfa, was opened 20 May 1913.[37] In the first service led by Dr William Edwards, Principal of the Baptist College in Cardiff, the key was handed to Miss Elliott, a faithful member at Tredegarville, and she had the honour of opening the new place of worship. The Rev. J. E. Roberts, Manchester, the successor of Dr Maclaren, delivered the inaugural sermon, and two hundred and eighty friends stayed for tea. The Rev. Grey Griffith, Tredegarville, presided over the evening meeting and addresses were given by the Rev. J. E. Roberts, Manchester, and the Rev. H. M. Hughes, Ebeneser, on behalf of the Free Church Council. The following day, Mr. W. Brace, MP, spoke in the afternoon meeting and the Rev. Grey Griffith, Tredegarville, in the evening meeting.[38]

The four stations opened under the direction of Alfred Tilley and confirmed by his successor James Baillie had made good, steady progress. During the first three years of Grey Griffiths' ministry, three of them became independent and the fourth a few years later. Forty-three members from Tredegarville formed the new cause at Llanishen in 1911:[39]

> In the following year, a further 136 members were dismissed to form the nucleus of the Baptist church at Pentyrch Street, a development of the work at the old 'Merthyr Street Mission'. Within two years another 118 members left to form the 'Maindy Baptist church', now known as Gabalfa. Thus in the first three years of the new ministry 297 members were dismissed to form independent causes in parts of the city.

The fourth station, Rumney, shared the ministry with St Mellons from 1921.

The old building was retained as a centre for youth work that was a new aspect of the church's work. While this was an encouragement, discouragement came with the War of 1914: 'Then came the 1914-18 War, which drained the church of about 100 young men, and those who were left, mostly elderly folk, carried on as best they could'.[40] The Maindy Barracks near the chapel 'was inundated with volunteers' and Gladstone school and other places turned into recruiting centres.[41] The pastor gained much experience in facing a smaller congregation, less workers and had the task of visiting homes in which members had been lost in the War. Little did he think then that he would also be involved in the Second World War.

CONFIRMING THE WORK
Before the War broke out, Caradoc Jones formed a successful Brotherhood in the Gabalfa church. In responding to a query by the Commissioners of 1911, John Morgan, a Cardiff solicitor, made the point that 'There is one feature in Cardiff with the English. In some of the chapels they have what they call brotherhoods, and popular

Sunday afternoon services in connection with their places of worship, and these are generally attended by adults'.[42] This was a positive contribution to the life of the church, but there was a negative aspect as well, because the men could not attend the Sunday school. It is not known, however, whether the Brotherhood in Gabalfa met on a Sunday or during the week, but it did prosper.[43]

The Brotherhood, or Men's Own as it was also called, was active for many years and about forty would attend. It is no surprise that numbers were low from 1914.[44] The Band of Hope showed no signs of weakening. Gabalfa, like so many churches in Wales, felt strongly about the bad effect that alcohol was having on so many people. One of the many Temperance movements was the Rechabites and they were strong in Gwent and East Glamorgan. By the beginning of the twentieth century the district had 6,000 members.[45] The children and the young ones in Gabalfa were taught concerning the principles of temperance. The Junior section numbered 20 in 1915 and the Senior section numbered 240. Apart from the Brotherhood and the Band of Hope, another significant aspect of the work was that of the Sunday school. The church itself had classes and it also opened a school in Conwil, so that there were 2 Sunday schools, 19 teachers and 388 scholars.[46]

A total of 118/9 had left Tredegarville to form the church at Gabalfa. There was steady growth for a number of years. Not only was the pastor full of energy, he also had faithful support from a good number of workers. Statistics for two years will indicate that growth:[47]

1914:

When formed	When settled	Bap.	Letters	Increase Profession	Restoration	Increase
1912	1907	36	18		1	47

1915:

1912	1907	29	16			34

Total: 1914 = 203; 1915 = 237

The figures are quite remarkable because they represent two years of the War period. Many of the men had left, but on the other hand many came to Cardiff to work in connection with the War and for other reasons as well. This is reflected in the high numbers that were received by letter. Even more significant is the number of those baptized. They would have been converted previously but it is not possible to say how many were converted in the church itself. They would have been baptized on confession of their faith, but there had been no conversions during those two years.

CONCERN FOR BRITTANY

By 1919, a concern that Caradoc Jones had since college days, laid heavily on his heart. As a Welshman, he knew something of the story of his fellow Celts. He had also met Saillens, Blocher and others from France, who were involved in some work in Brittany. In accepting the call to Cardiff, Caradoc Jones had made it clear to the church that if God called him to Brittany, he would respond as soon as possible. He had a strong conviction that the Roman Catholic Church was keeping the people in bondage and that its teaching was contrary to Scripture.[48] He had even applied to the Baptist Missionary Society, but was told that he was too old to learn two languages, that is, French and Breton. The Society did arrange for him to visit Morlaix. The visit convinced Caradoc Jones that this was not the particular area of service for him but did not give specific reasons for coming to that conclusion.[49] On the human level Morlaix was attractive. It was an established work and one of the missionaries there was a descendant of John Jenkins, Hengoed, who established the cause in 1835, after visiting in 1834.[50]

In the spring o 1919, Caradoc Jones attended the May meetings of the London Baptist Association and the annual conference at Spurgeon's College. At the College the Welsh Quartette of the Revival period was reconstructed to sing 'Worthy the Lamb'. Among the company in the May meetings were Dr McCaig, his former Principal at Spurgeon's College, and E. A Carter, secretary of the Pioneer Mission. Caradoc Jones shared his burden with the two men and asked them: 'Are you doing anything about Brittany?'[51] At that time the Pioneer Mission knew that there was an opening in Paimpol. Both McCaig and Carter and Charles Phillips, Treasurer of the Mission, had already visited the town. When Caradoc Jones asked his question the three men realized that the pastor of Gabalfa could be the right person for Paimpol. They arranged a visit for Caradoc Jones, believing that this would be a great help for him in considering his future. During the stay, Caradoc Jones became more convinced than ever that God was calling him, not only to Brittany, but specifically to Paimpol. He informed the Pioneer Mission that he was willing to go to Brittany.[52]

Caradoc Jones wanted to solve one problem before leaving for Paimpol. Members and friends had responded well to the building appeal, and £2,000 had been collected during the opening day. Since that time the gifts came in but they were not so numerous and not substantial. A sum of £386 still remained and the pastor did not want to leave before that sum was cleared.[53] He made it a matter of prayer and thought at first that he would ask for a particular sum, part of the total. He realized that this revealed a lack of faith and believed that he should pray for the whole sum to be cleared. A deaconess at Gabalfa mentioned the name of a ship owner and suggested to the pastor that it would be worth paying the gentleman a visit. Caradoc

Jones did not know that person but felt that God was speaking to him through the deaconess and went to see him. When asked what he needed, Caradoc Jones replied: 'I need £386 to clear the debt on my church'.[54] Without any discussion the ship owner said that he would clear the debt because he was on the point of selling one of his ships. The ship was not sold but the ship owner's promise was honoured and the last obstacle on the way to Brittany had been removed.

On 11 April 1920, a thanksgiving service was held when the large congregation at Gabalfa joined in praise to God for meeting their material needs during the past seven years.[55] Seven years seemed a long time to clear the debt. Not so long if it is borne in mind that they included four years of war. They had known the hand of God upon them, both materially and spiritually.

Caradoc Jones was now in a position to prepare for going to Brittany. Farewell and thanksgiving services were held the end of April and the beginning of May 1920. During the thanksgiving service, a tablet was unveiled that was an expression of the congregation's gratitude for a faithful ministry:[56]

> On leaving for missionary work in Brittany, the church desires to place on record its love and esteem for their first Pastor, Caradoc Jones. His sterling character, his self-sacrificing whole-hearted ministry and for that faith and enterprise through which the building was erected, and by his untiring efforts the building debt liquidated in seven years.
>
> 'Other sheep I have which are not of this fold'.

As one reporter said, Cardiff was losing a man of vision, courage and faith.[57]

The induction service took place in the Metropolitan Tabernacle, London.[58] It was held on a Monday, prayer meeting night at the Tabernacle. The pastor presided and a number of Pioneer Mission representatives were present. A Member form Gabalfa, Cardiff, bore witness to the faithful, persevering work of Caradoc Jones, and he replied briefly. The pastor of the Metropolitan Tabernacle 'gave a cordiall farewell on behalf of the congregation and himself', basing his message on Psalm 121, verse 8, 'The Lord shall preserve thy going out and thy coming in from this time forth, and for evermore'.[59]

Caradoc Jones was ready to leave for Brittany under the auspices of the Pioneer Mission.

THE PIONEER MISSION

The founder was E. A. Carter, a former Spurgeon College student.[60] When he left the College in 1882, he spent a few years in the pastoral ministry and during that time realized the need for pioneering work. He himself, his brother F. C. Carter and his wife, H. H. Farmer and Mr. Chamberlain, a gospel singer, committed themselves to pioneering work. They prepared a plan of campaign and presented it to C. H. Spurgeon. At first he did not think that the time was right for such a project, but because of the zeal of the missionaries and the clear plan they had, Spurgeon gave his support, 'remaining its constant friend until his death'.[61] Apart from Spurgeon, other supporters included Archibald G. Brown, London, and Richard Cory, member of Tredegarville Baptist church, Cardiff. Support also came from the Prospective Chapel sites Syndicate, set up by F. C. Carter in conjunction with the Home Counties Baptist Association.[62]

The Pioneer Mission was interested in work at home and abroad. It supported work in Germany and Holland and it was the Mission that urged William Fetler, Caradoc Jones' friend, to return to Russia. A link had been forged with Paris through Reuben Saillens and his son in law A. Blocher. They attended Pioneer Mission meetings in London and were interested in the work in Brittany. Caradoc Jones knew both of them through those meetings and the meetings of the College.

The main details concerning the Pioneer Mission can be summarized:[63]

Objects: To glorify God 1. By preaching the gospel and winning souls, and where necessary making a work permanent by forming a Baptist Church. 2. By resuscitating weak and struggling churches. 3 By General Mission and Caravan work in villages.

Sphere: In new, increasing and needy places and countries, wherever God opens the way [Brittany 1920; Spain 1921].

Needs: 1. Prayer of God's people. 2. Subscriptions and donations. 3. Sum of money for chapel building, either as a gift to the Loan Fund or at a small interest.

The Pioneer Mission, therefore, concentrated on pioneering work and helping weak churches. It was church centred. The Mission emphasized personal salvation and also emphasized the need to bring individual believers into the fellowship of the church. The churches that were formed should be baptismal in belief and practice. Caradoc Jones agreed whole-heartedly with the aims of the Pioneer Mission and was ready to be its missionary in Brittany.

1. 'Notes', *The Sword and the Trowel,* September, December 1907; 'Settlement', June 1906.
2. Peter Finch, *Real Cardiff* (Seren Press, Bridgend, 2004 ed.), 10.
3. John Davies, *Hanes Cymru* (Allen Lane, The Penguin Press, 1990), 453.
4. David Jenkins, *Shipowners of Cardiff* (Cardiff, 1997), Appendix 5.
5. Dennis Morgan, *The Illustrated History of Cardiff Suburbs* (Breedon Books, 2003), 64.
6. *Royal Commission on the Church of England* (1911), vol. 1V, book III, 41109.
7. Ibid. 41098.
8. J. A. Jenkins and R. Edwards James, *The History of Nonconformity in Cardiff* (London, 1901), 88, 176.
9. *Royal Commission on the Church of England, 1911,* vol. 1V, book III, 41202, 41252.
10. Geraint Fielder, *Grace, Gut and Gumption* (Christian Focus, The Evangelical Movement of Wales, 2000), especially 67-110.
11. A history of the church, T. H. Hill, *The Tredegarville Story* (1961).
12. Cory family, *Burke's Landed Gentry* (1937), 489-490. The Cory Hall used to

be a very important centre in Cardiff. It was demolished to build the Capitol Shopping Centre.

13. *On the Wings of the Dove*, 104, 203; Harriet Cadot, *Recollections of an earnest life* [1907].
14. *Jubilee of the Tredegarville Baptist Church Cardiff, 1861-1911* (1961), 19.
15. *On the Wings of the Dove*, 104.
16. *Jubilee of the Tredegarville Baptist Church*, 20.
17. Ibid.
18. Ibid., 21.
19. Ibid.
20. Ibid.
21. Jenkins and James, *The History of Nonconformity in Cardiff*, 143.
22. Hill, *Tredegarville Story*, 17.
23. *Royal Commission 1911*, vol. V1, Appendices to Minutes of Evidence.
24. Glamorgan Record Office: *Handbook 1909*, DD/Bap 23.
25. *Knight in Royal Service*, 18.
26. Census, 1901; Criddle Family Genealogy Forum: viewed 14/10/05.
27. Census, 1901; *Handbook*, 1909, 1911.
28. *Handbook*, 1909, 1911.
29. *Knight in Royal Service*, 17.
30. Ibid.
31. Gabalfa &Maindy Baptist Church, Bazaar Programme.
32. *Handbook*, 1907, 1909.
33. *Knight in Royal Service*, 17.
34. Ibid.
35. Bazaar Programme.
36. *Knight in Royal Service*, 18.
37. 'Gabalfa Baptist Church', *South Wales Daily News*, 21 May 1913.
38. Ibid.
39. Hill, *Tredegarville Story*, 18.
40. *Knight in Royal Service*, 18.
41. Dennis Morgan, *Illustrated History of Cardiff Suburbs*, 43.
42. *Royal Commission, 1911*, vol. 1V, book III, 41173.
43. Glamorgan Record Office: Report East Glamorgan English Baptist Association, 1913-4, 1915.
44. Ibid.
45. R. Tudur Jones, *Faith and Crisis of a Nation* (Cardiff, 2004), 398-9.
46. East Glamorgan Association, Report.
47. Ibid.
48. *Knight in Royal Service*, 19.
49. Ibid.
50. T. M. Bassett, *The Baptists of Wales and the Missionary Society*, 60-2.
51. *Knight in Royal Service*, 20.
52. Ibid.
53. Ibid.
54. Ibid.

55. Ibid., 21.
56. Ibid.
57. 'Rhos', *Rhos Herald*, 15 May 1920.
58. 'The Pioneer Mission', *The Sword and Trowel*, June 1920.
59. Ibid.
60. History of the Mission, 'Survey of the History of the Pioneer Mission from its Commencement in 1889', *Pioneer Review*, October-December, 1935.
61. Ibid.
62. Ibid.
63. Printed on the front page of *The Pioneer Review* on a number of occasions.

4

DOING SOMETHING FOR BRITTANY
1920-29

Caradoc Jones went to Brittany under the auspices of the Pioneer
Mission, but the work in Paimpol was pioneered by the Society of
Friends, the Quakers. They were missionary minded and they had a
work in France and Madagascar.

BACKGROUND
The Quaker, Charles Dickinson Terrell from Bristol, had heard of a
group in Brittany that was praying for an evangelist to be sent to
them. He and his wife, Mable, arrived in Brittany in 1904. They
arrived in La Rochelle in 1904, and stayed there for a brief period
before moving to Paimpol, Brittany. They also worked in
Lézardrieux.[1] They found a home and also a cottage where they
could hold meetings. One home that welcomed them was that of
Madame Masclet, who was to become the first member of the
church.[2] A tin Tabernacle was built in 1905, pulled down in 1913 and
a building erected in what is now known as rue de Gras Plat. The
Terrells ministered in the Mission Hall, in the town, and visited the
fishing schooners. They presented New Testaments, Gospels and
Temperance literature to all the schooners.[3]

Occasional meetings were held at Plourivo, Plouezec, Pontrieux,
Bréhat, Le Questel and Ste Barbe. Both husband and wife worked
diligently, but the Great War of 1914-1918 greatly hampered the
work. By 1919, Charles Terrell, because of health and family reasons,

retired. He continued to keep in touch with Paimpol and visited the place quite often.

The Tabernacle, Paris, was in continual contact with the Pioneer Mission, and was always at hand to support the witness of the Mission in Brittany. The Mission was also helping Tabernacle as it was contributing financially to the building of a new church in the Montmatre area of Paris. Arthur Blocher of the Tabernacle was also chairman of a committee, of which Terrell was a member, reconstituting a 'sister mission' at Tremel. Blocher urged the Mission to send a man to take over the work in Paimpol.[4] Both the Church in Paris and Mission were of one mind, doctrinally, and were worried that there were signs of deviating from the evangelical faith amongst the Baptists in France. In 1921, the Baptists in France divided into two; one group forming a Federation and an another group forming an Association. Arthur Blocher and the people at Tabernacle did not join either the Federation or the Association. They remained as an independent church.[5]

The Paimpol church was situated in an area away from the centre of the town. In the town itself, the old and the new can still be seen side by side, the sixteenth century houses, the old Roman Catholic church and the more modern houses and shops. The old streets open to the sea that has a fascination for the people of Paimpol, because until the early 1930s, cod fishing was the mainstay of the people. The men would leave for long periods to Iceland and the shores of Newfoundland. The Widow's Cross still reminds the inhabitants of the days when the women would gather there, anxiously, hoping that the men would return safely.[6] By the time the trade had come to an end, about two thousand men had lost their lives at sea. There is a memorial to them in the Memorial Chapel in rue Saint-Vincent, and in the cemetery at Ploubazlanec.[7]

The lobster took the place of the cod, but fishing is still carried on as a leisure activity. The pleasure boats have taken the place of the fishing boats and sailing attracts many of the visitors to Paimpol.

Very different from fish is the cocoa bean, introduced from South Africa in 1928. The town had a weekly market when those from surrounding areas would come in to sell the produce of the land. In matters of religion, most of the people are still staunch Roman Catholics and the church dominates the town, geographically and spiritually. When Caradoc Jones arrived in Paimpol it would be possible to hear some Breton being spoken, but the French Government's anti-Breton policy made it unpopular for the people to speak the language. French was the official language and Breton was forbidden in schools and public places. Signs could be seen in public places: 'Spitting on the floor and speaking Breton prohibited'.[8] Some efforts were being made to revive the language and to keep alive Breton dress and customs. It was a story that would be very familiar to a Welshman.

EARLY DAYS

Caradoc Jones was always ready to be on the offensive. He knew that there was much opposition to Protestant work in Brittany and, therefore, he would have to be wise as well as being aggressive. At the end of four months in Paimpol he was ready to arrange a nine-day mission. Colporteur and evangelist Huck joined him in the venture. Adolph Huck, from Paris, had worked as assistant cook in London. [9] Someone gave him a gospel tract and he read it with interest, as he was a disappointed Roman Catholic. A little later a Frenchman invited him to a meeting and Huck responded positively. The service was the means of his conversion. On his return to Paris he joined the rue de Lille Church (Tabernacle). When Charles Terrell retired, Blocher arranged for Huck to go to Paimpol. He had been there for a few months before Caradoc Jones arrived.[10]

The new pastor believed that it was time to look for a harvest, because faithful sowing had been carried out for a number of years in terms of preaching, Sunday school and a school on Thursday. According to Caradoc Jones there was a need to be more open. It was time to challenge Paimpol and the neighbourhood with the gospel.[11] Charles Terrell, Dr McCaig, London, the two Jenkinses from Morlaix[12] and Arthur Blocher joined the pastor and the colporteur. The meetings were widely advertised in the town and a poster was set up on the gate of the colporteur's home. The town council gave permission to hold open-air services in the Market Place, 'which is a thing little short of the miraculous to all who know France and Brittany'. [13] As he had a musical gift, Caradoc Jones trained a choir to sing in the open-air services and he himself played a Bilhorn portable organ.

The singing attracted large crowds, while many listened at doors and windows. Many of the listeners attended the meetings at the Mission Hall. Six meetings were held in Paimpol itself and two each at Ste Barbe and Lan Baston. The last meeting was tested and about forty people expressed a desire to stand for Christ making the total of sixty for the series. Pastor Blocher took part in the last meeting and was delighted with what he saw and heard.[14]

All of those involved in the Mission were strengthened in their faith and were more prepared to continue with their witness in Paimpol. It was generally acknowledged that it was Caradoc Jones' venturesome spirit that had led the way. This was acknowledged in Brittany and London. After returning to London, Dr McCaig referred to the Mission in *The Pioneer Review*:[15]

> It was largely due to the consecrated ingenuity and courage of Mr. Jones, and has touched the neighbourhood in a manner undreamed of by the most sanguine. We had the great pleasure of taking a small part in it, and witnessing the interest manifested by the people of Paimpol and the outlying villages, and we can testify that Mr. Terrell does not exaggerate the matter in his report.

The report of Mr Terrell summarized the main events of the mission, marvelling at what had been accomplished and urgently asking for prayer to continue witnessing in Paimpol. Dr Saillens, Paris, held some meetings in April 1922 and his ministry strengthened the faith of believers and challenged the unbelievers.[16]

Outside Preachers from outside of Paimpol helped a little with the ministry, but the burden of the work was on the shoulders of the regular workers. Caradoc Jones himself left for a while to follow a language course in Paris, but Huck and Charles Terrell, who was in Paimpol for a brief period, persevered in the pastor's absence.[17] Terrell arranged extra prayer meetings but was disappointed when only four persons turned up for the first one. Encouragement was on the way because in the last meeting that Terrell attended before leaving, there were twenty-four people present. It was difficult to hold meetings on cold, dark nights, when the country roads were unlighted and muddy. The brave worshippers had to bring their lanterns with them to be a light to their path.[18]

Terrell emphasized home visiting. He believed that it was an essential part of the mission in Paimpol and district. He would take a number of gospel tracts with him and, if at all possible, would speak concerning the content of a tract. Terrell visited those living a fair distance away from Paimpol and held meetings in some homes. He was impressed with the fact that there was family worship in some of them. He identified one real need, that of a motor car, that would make it easier to travel and enable the pastor and the evangelist to spend more time with individuals and families.[19]

Caradoc Jones returned from Paris and resumed the leadership of the church.[20] He was finding the languages, both French and Breton, difficult, but the course in Paris did help a little. One way of making progress was by translating hymns from English and Welsh to French and Breton. At the same time it was possible to develop congregational singing in the church. By 1922, Caradoc Jones had edited a small collection of hymns: *Cantiques Evangéliques*, consisting of thirty-eight hymns and twenty choruses. Most of the hymns were in French with a few in Breton. The editor included two of his own compositions, one being an imitation and fourteen imitations in the Chorus section. Some of the choruses were well known in Wales during the 1904-5 Revival, including 'Blessed assurance' and 'O the Lamb, the dying Lamb'. His fondness for Reuben Saillens is revealed and in a later collection a high number of his hymns were included.[21]

The missionary and his helpers visited the homes and the shops, and talked with those they met on the street.[22] They were surprised that so many accepted a Scripture and even more surprised when they heard that a few priests were ignoring the Scriptural texts found in some of the homes. Other priests were not so tolerant. As far as they were concerned, there was only one religion for Brittany, that of Rome. Not surprisingly, therefore, it was a source of great joy to the witnesses to come across a husband and wife who had been recently converted. Converts in the evangelical sense were walking the thronged Roman Catholic streets of Paimpol.[23]

Although Caradoc Jones was ready to be on the offensive, he realized that he had to map out his campaigns very carefully. A railway ran from Guingamp to Paimpol and to Plouha on the coast. A railway linked Plouha and St Brieuc and a line was being constructed between Paimpol and Treguier. There was, therefore, a triangle within which the church could concentrate its energies. Within that triangle, on the coast, were Lézardrieux, Kerity, Plouezec, Plouha and Etables. Inland were Plourivo, Pontrieux, Lanvollon and Châtelaudren. Only Paimpol and St Brieuc had settled ministries. There were open doors but Caradoc Jones knew that wherever an open door is found, there are also many adversaries.[24]

Caradoc Jones and his people were conscious of hindrances, apart from the Roman Catholic environment. The Protestant building was tucked away from the centre of the town. They knew of instances when visitors had failed to find the church. A church near the centre of the town would make a real difference to the work, and, also, a permanent home for the pastor. Some services had been held in Ste Barbe but at the end of September 1922 the evangelist had to leave his home and at that time had nowhere to go. A room had been rented at Lanbastan, but there was uncertainty as to how long the arrangement would last. The answer would be a new mission hall.

Caradoc Jones appealed for money but the greatest need was for men filled with the Spirit of God:[25]

> But greater than all other needs is the need for Spirit-filled men to come and enter these open doors; to come and till the open field; to come and consolidate the centre and captivate those outlying towns and villages for Christ.

God's work was to be done in the power of God's Spirit.

HELP AND SUPPORT

There was no immediate response to Caradoc Jones' call for workers, but some help was at hand. Pastor Blocher continued to support the church at Paimpol, a few churches from England and help came from Wales. A great deal of enthusiasm was created amongst some of the churches in Cardiff. Caradoc Jones, as a former pastor of Gabalfa Baptist church, was in contact not only with that church but other churches in the city as well. Through his initiative meetings were set up in the city that led to an annual meeting and other activities to promote the Pioneer Mission's witness in Paimpol.[26]

In 1922 three Cardiff Baptist churches, Gabalfa, Splott Road and Tabernacle, Welsh Baptist, arranged a convention in Splott Road. Caraduc Jones was present, addressed the meeting and reached 'Great heights of impassioned earnestness as he spoke again on Brittany'.[27] The other speakers were Dr. McCaig, assuring the support of Spurgeon's College to the work and R. B. Jones, Porth, Rhondda, one of the prominent leaders of the 1904 5 Revival in Wales. R. B., as he was called, was an enthusiastic champion of mission work abroad. This convention led to the formation of other conventions in other places in south Wales.[28]

Another expression of support was the Garden Party and Sale held in the gardens of the charming residence of Lord Pontypridd, who was an admirer of Caradoc Jones.[29] Apart from the three churches already mentioned five other churches joined the activity of the Garden Party: Hope, Canton; Connell Road; Longcross; Eldon Road, and Salem, Welsh Baptist, Splott. A pattern of Garden Parties and conventions was established. Such activity realized prayer and financial support. Groups and churches prayed for Paimpol and collections were made in different meetings. Supporters responded to particular needs. The pastor needed a car and the church at Paimpol wanted to move to another building. Examples of responses were:[30]

Brittany Motor Car:			
Cardiff Garden Party 'Bronwydd'	£27	0	0
Paimpol, Tabernacle:			
Cardiff Garden Party 'Bronwydd'	£87	10	0
Cardiff Garden Sale, Mrs Morgan	£25	0	0
Friends at Paimpol	£ 21	0	0

Eighty-seven pounds was quite a substantial gift at that time. Occasionally the annual gifts from Cardiff reached two hundred pounds. The Cory family continued to be liberal in their giving.[31]

One of the leading organizers of the Garden Party was Mrs J. Richards, but Mrs Morgan, Cardiff, arranged another one on a lesser scale.[32] Other supporters appeared during this period, including Mr and Mrs Morgan Davies, members at Tabernacle, Welsh Baptist church.[33] Apart from prayer and giving they helped in a different ways. Mademoiselle Coquin, a Roman Catholic, had been converted under Caradoc Jones' ministry. She was anxious to widen her experience and wanted to master the English language before entering the College at Nogent sur Marne, Paris. Caradoc Jones arranged for her to stay in Cardiff, with Mr and Mrs Morgan Davies. During her stay she attended the Sunday school at Tabernacle. When she left, the scholars and teachers presented her with a French Bible.[34]

Morgan Davies and his wife had already visited Paimpol.[35] They did not visit just to enjoy themselves, they went there to be active during their stay. This was a valuable contribution that they and others made to the life of the church at Paimpol. A number of individuals and representatives of churches spent different periods of time and helped in whatever way possible. An opportune time was the holiday period. Some stayed for a few days while others stayed for a week or two. A group of five from Wales, and two from the Bible Institute, Nogent sur Marne, helped during a holiday in 1924.[36] The following year, Caradoc Jones welcomed a delegation from the Welsh Wesleyan Church. He met the delegation at St Brieuc, where they held services on the Sunday.[37] On Monday, Pastor Scarabin brought them to Paimpol, where he spoke in Breton and preached in French. The Wesleyans brought greetings from Wales and shared fellowship with the congregation and the eight pastors that were present. Three of the delegation joined with Caradoc Jones to form a quartette and sang twice 'to the joy of all present'.[38]

During the same year, 1925, a Frenchman, an Englishman and two Welshmen stayed for a while to help with the work. [39] The following year French, Swiss, English and Welsh believers stayed for a brief period to share in the witness of the gospel. A French Pastor and Evangelist took part, an English missionary for Morocco, and a Welsh Pastor.[40] The pastor had bought a number of hymn-tunes and when Mrs Richards and Mrs J. Richards, both from Cardiff, arrived early in 1928, they helped Caradoc Jones to teach the congregation some of the well-known Welsh hymns. [41] The pastor was always ready to include music in the worship but emphasized that it was a means to praise God. It could also be a witness to the message of the gospel of the Lord Jesus Christ.

BAPTISMS, WEDDINGS AND FUNERALS

A number of events marked the differences between the Protestant and Roman Catholic faiths. A Protestant baptism, wedding and funeral appeared very strange to those brought up strictly in the Catholic Faith. Their significance illustrated the wide gap between the two traditions. Caradoc Jones held a strong conviction concerning believer's baptism. Although baptism was not necessary for salvation it 'was necessary to full obedience of the command of the Lord'.[42] The claim that a baby could be brought into membership of the Church through baptism was anathema to him. The first person to ask for baptism was Madame Masclet (né Menage), who was the first lady to be received into membership by Charles Terrell.[43] She was born in Dunkirk in 1859, the daughter of a sea captain. He was a hard man and opposed to any form of religion. She, however, attended the Roman Catholic Church and contemplated entering a Convent, but she met Monsieur Jarlegon and they married. They settled in Morbihan Department and had two children, but in a short time she lost her husband and both of the children.

Madame Masclet moved to Havre where she married Monsieur Masclet a friend of her first husband. Because of her husband's ill health they had to move to Lézardrieux, Brittany, where he died. Madame Masclet returned to Havre where she was given a New Testament and heard of the Salvation Army: 'having heard much from friends of the Salvation Army, she finally decided to attend a half-night of prayer there, disguised in a big shawl'. This led to her conversion, and shortly she joined the 'Army' and became a Salvationist.

Madame Masclet's sister lived in Lézardrieux and when she died she left two children without anyone to care for them. Madame Masclet returned to Brittany to care for the two children. They lived in the upper room of a large house in Kirminguy and it became a calling place for Christian workers. The home was also open for services, held in a wooden hall that was part of the house. She also helped Chapallez, a member in Paimpol, with the work at Plougrescant.[44]

It was during a visit to Bournemouth that she was led to consider believer's baptism. After discussing the matter with friends and reading the New Testament she became convinced that the way forward was to be baptized, but on her return to Paimpol. The ordinance took place in the sea at Poulafret during the winter of 1923, in spite of the cold weather and the condition of Madame Masclet's health. A young girl of eighteen, who had been converted during Dr Saillens' visit to Paimpol, joined Madame Masclet for baptism.[45]

Caradoc Jones and the other organizers had made note of the times of the tides and had arranged the baptism accordingly. Before the ordinance the pastor preached a sermon in the church on believer's baptism; the first in Paimpol. He announced the arrangements explaining that the candidates would follow in a wagonette. They arrived half and hour late because the wagoner had forgotten the change from summer to normal time. The horse and carriage were two feet deep in water when they reached the appointed place of baptism. Apart from the congregation there were three men in a boat nearby in a light-hearted mood, but when they heard the testimony of Madame Masclet and saw her entering the water, they were silenced and removed their hats. Caradoc Jones was responsible for baptizing the candidates and his voice rang across the waters as he shouted: 'On confession of thy faith, I baptize thee in the Name of the Father, Son and Holy Ghost'.[46] He himself sent an account of the event to the *Pioneer Review*:[47]

A silent immersion, a solemn uprising to the sounds of the Doxology from those who could sing-the most were in tears, and above all before reaching the shore the Halelluja cry of Madame Masclet repeated again and again. Our young sister robed in white, stepped bravely into the water, and again the same solemn words, and same solemn rite, the same joyous praise and a new flood of tears – and the first Baptismal service at Paimpol was over; but not its influençe.

In their curiosity, many Roman Catholics were present and were so impressed that they promised to come to the next baptism. Another lady of sixty years of age was baptized as the result of being convinced of the need during a Communion service.

The church had contacts in the Baudic Lighthouse and one Wednesday four carloads made their way there to hold a service and to baptize.[48] Two sisters lived in the Lighthouse, one, the oldest Protestant in Paimpol, and the other the wife of a converted infidel who had just recently died. A very representative crowd gathered for the occasion; a family from Paris, two families from St Brieuc, members from Paimpol, a missionary from Morocco and the Lighthouse family. After the service the two candidates were baptized in the river Trieux. They 'entered the water joyfully, and emerged praising God with a loud voice for his grace and mercy'.[49]

Very few weddings were celebrated during the early period in Paimpol. In 1923 a nominal Roman Catholic was married to a Protestant lady. According to the account 'It was a most impressive service'.[50] Referring to a later wedding, Caradoc Jones mentioned two customs in the Protestant churches. One was the custom of presenting a Bible to the married couple and the other was described thus: 'They have another nice custom worth copying by English churches, namely that the chief bridesmaid, seconded by the best man, takes up a collection for the church. She always does it charmingly while he bashfully follows from seat to seat and hardly does anything but looks on helplessly. This was duly done, and the result over five pounds to the work of the church!'[51] Even, as a bachelor, Caradoc Jones hoped for two weddings a week.

A Protestant funeral was a real attraction for the Roman Catholic community. There were two early examples of note. The first was that of a former police inspector from Paris. He came to live in Brittany and was afraid that after his death, friends or neighbours would call a priest to be in charge of the funeral. He, therefore, made a personal, written declaration:[52]

> To Monsieur, the Pastor of the Evangelical Church of Paimpol.
> On April 26th 1921, I being reconciled to God by the aid of the Holy Spirit, and by the intermediary of the representative of the Evangelical Baptist Church
> I give full powers to Monsieur the Pastor of the said Church to dispose of my mortal remains after my death, so as to be buried by him when my Saviour shall call me to pass through the Valley of Shadow of Death.
> As to my soul, I remit it into the hands of our Lord Jesus Christ, Amen.

The gentleman died two years later. In the funeral service Caradoc Jones related the conversion story of the former police inspector. At the graveside Rev. H. Jenkins, Morlaix, spoke on the blessedness of those who die in the Lord.[53]

The other example is of a person who in his young days attended Sunday school during Charles Terrell's ministry.[54] The young man rebelled against the gospel, shook off all restraints and lived just to please himself. His behaviour became wild and at times would threaten the life of his mother. Marriage did not change him at all. Caradoc Jones visited the man when he was taken ill, but after a few visits the pastor was no longer welcomed. It was a surprise to the church, therefore, when they heard that the man had refused to see the priest and had asked for Charles Terrell, who was in Paimpol at the time. Terrell and Caradoc Jones visited the sick person who told them that he had trusted Christ for salvation and desired a Protestant funeral. He made his desire in writing with his wife, mother and Madame Masclet as witnesses. When he died there was a good congregation at the funeral service in the chapel although some of the deceased's family refused to attend. The mourners even sang at the graveside. It was reported that a priest was hiding behind the wall to witness the event. The rumour was spread abroad that the Protestants had paid 500 francs for his body.[55]

NEW WORKERS

A few more workers joined Caradoc Jones, and, consequently it was possible for him to give more attention to areas outside Paimpol. The Rev. E. Jenkins, son and grandson of the pioneer of the work in Morlaix, came for twelve months. It was a service in Paimpol, and meeting Caradoc Jones, that led E. Jenkins to Spurgeon's College and then back to Morlaix. During the brief period in Paimpol he was 'Missionary Pastor'. He had to leave because of health problems.[56] Mademoiselle Coquin,[57] the lady who had been to Cardiff, had finished her course in Nogent sur Marne and was waiting for an opening to mission work. As she was staying in Paimpol for an unknown length of time, she was made a deaconess. Another newcomer that was welcomed was the car provided for the pastor. Friends covered the expenses and gifts sent included a substantial one from Cardiff.[58]

It was with great joy that Caradoc Jones welcomed two new helpers from Wales, Arthur Matthews from Cardiff (1899-1980) recommended by Mrs Morgan, the Mount, Cardiff,[59] and Edna Jones from Ponciau, the pastor's niece. [60] She had spent some time in Middlesbrough but when her father died she returned to Ponciau. She and her mother were invited to Paimpol for a holiday. The mother could not go, but another relative accompanied Edna Jones to Paimpol. As the result of the holiday Edna Jones returned there to keep house for her uncle.[61] This was an answer to a pressing need for it was very difficult for the pastor to find lodgings. It was much easier to find a place with someone looking after him.

Charles Phillips of the Pioneer Mission visited during 1928 and, because Edna Jones had arrived, it was possible for him to stay with the pastor and his niece. On the first evening, Charles Phillip visited the Bible study at Paimpol, where about sixty were present. The singing was hearty and there was a healthy spiritual atmosphere. Friday morning Caradoc Jones accompanied Charles Phillips to Kerity to see the Protestant graves in the churchyard.[62]

The destination on Saturday evening was St Rion, where the meeting was held in a large, very dirty room with an earthen floor. Charles Phillips gave a brief message to a congregation of about sixty. Sunday was busy. Sunday school was held at 10 o'clock and about thirty attended. The afternoon service was at 2 o'clock and at 4 o'clock they joined the Open-Air Mission Motor Caravan for a meeting.[63]

MISSIONS
Arthur Matthews arrived to join the ongoing work in Paimpol and to visit the surrounding villages.[64] He joined Caradoc Jones in a number of evangelistic missions. The church had been looking for an opening in Lézardrieux. After a long wait, a Gospel Van arrived there to hold meetings in the open-air and distribute Scriptures. Some from the Paimpol church joined the team for a while, and they succeeded in establishing a work in that place. The real problem was to find a building to hold meetings. Arthur Matthews made inquiries about a suitable place but he was told that about twenty people were interested in the building and that the chances that a Protestant having it were slim indeed. Arthur Matthews found another place but the rent was two hundred francs a night, a sum that the Paimpol church could not afford. It was quite a surprise therefore when the proprietor sent a letter to the church, offering the place for twenty francs a night, plus lighting, benches and chairs. The offer was gratefully received.[65]

A series of four meetings was arranged. The Paimpol group, including the choir, travelled in a charabanc and, as they were approaching the Hall for the first meeting, they sang hymns joyfully. Their spirits dropped when they entered the Hall because just one person had arrived. The group started singing and a few people came in until, eventually, a few dozen had gathered together. The purpose of the meeting was explained and the people listened well and, when the hymns were given out, joined in the singing. The missionaries promised to return for Christmas and before the end of the first series, the town crier was already announcing the coming visit to those coming from the Mass. The same group intended visiting another part of the town in January 1929.[66]

The witnesses were anxious, not only to find a place to preach, but, also, a place where somebody might live and settle down amongst the people. They started looking for such a place. The choir members had paid half of their travelling expenses and were willing to keep to this arrangement.[67]

The second mission of the period was to the town of Loquivy. There had been opposition to the gospel in this place and Charles Terrell and his helpers had been chased out of the town by infuriated women, instigated it was believed by two Sisters of Mercy. The only place available was a loft and they had to climb a rickety ladder to reach it. Homes had been visited beforehand.[68]

The company arrived late for the first meeting because of a puncture to one of the wheels of the charabanc. They arrived eventually:[69]

> We climbed into the loft, and found there a table on fish-boxes, half a dozen planks for seats, and a few fish-boxes along the side of the room. There was no chance of anyone being at ease in Zion! We were soon followed by a number of people, until we were about a hundred and fifty and, wonder of wonders in theses days, more men than women.

All present were asked to take off their hats and not to smoke during the service. Hymn-sheets, New Testament and the one Bible that the evangelists had with them, were sold at the end of the meeting.

Arthur Matthews preached on the second night and again the people listened well. One lady declared that she had become a Protestant the previous evening. As on the previous evening, hymn-sheets and New Testaments were sold. The team was three quarters of an hour late for the third meeting due to the charabanc breaking down, but the people were waiting for them: 'A bigger crowd than ever was awaiting us-half the village was out-the room was packed, many being pinned to the sides and doorposts. We turned the meeting into a praise and testimony one'. [70] No wonder that the team felt happy; the gospel had been preached and many Scriptures had reached many individuals and many homes. The venture was well worth the extra expenditure. Response was not so spontaneous and enthusiastic in the third town that was visited. There were two main reasons for such a response. The area was strongly Roman Catholic and the room were the meetings were held was not heated. Nearly thirty people from Paimpol went there faithfully for three nights.[71]

In spite of difficulties there were encouragements. On a Sunday after the mission, one person walked for five miles to the services in Paimpol, while another walked seven miles to attend meetings led by Arthur Matthews. He returned to the place of the mission and was met with strong opposition but was welcomed in a few homes.[72] According to Arthur Matthews, this was to be expected because the division of the people was quite clear. According to the missionary, there were three groups: declared anti-religionists, staunch Roman Catholics and Roman Catholics that were sympathetic to the Protestant faith. Arthur Matthews had come to this conclusion after visiting from door to door. Those of the third group were not numerous in that area. When he visited another area where a mission had been held: 'I found that the special Mission work had proved a great aid to the visitation work, for the attitude of the villagers was decidedly changed in our favour after the Mission'.[73]

One of the helpers in the missions was Mademoiselle Deleu. She had been converted and baptized when on holiday at Paimpol.[74] After spending two years in the College at Nogent sur Marne, she returned to Paimpol waiting for an opening in the Ivory Coast. While waiting she was made a deaconess and gave herself zealously to various aspects of the work. Apart from personal work and working with the women, she had taught the children at the Le Palus Orphanage. The opening to Africa came in 1929. A moving farewell service was held in which Madame Masclet made the presentation to Mademoiselle Deleu on behalf of the church.[75]

The church suffered another loss when Sister Noel returned to her home in Rion. She continued to visit Paimpol occasionally in spite of the six-mile journey. She would walk part of the way to cut down on expenses and took a train for the other part of the journey. She was sorry that she could only visit when the weather was favourable and made her best to visit before winter arrived.[76]

A number of females supported the work in Paimpol and there was also a Women's Auxiliary. It was formed in 1922, with Mrs E. A. Carter as president. Included in the list of vice-presidents were Mrs Thomas Spurgeon and Miss Beatrice Cory, Cardiff.[77] Beatrice Cory was maintaining the support of the family to the Pioneer Mission, by prayer and liberal giving. The Auxiliary sent regular gifts to the Mission in Paimpol, especially to Madame Masclet and drew attention to particular needs in the reports. A report of 1929 refers to the workers:[78]

Madame Huck	supported by the Mission
Madame Masclet	had been most zealous, but was now caring for three small orphan children. She witnessed regularly to those visiting the children.
Madame Matthews	a young Breton convert. Since her marriage to Arthur Matthews worked part time. Living at the time in St Quay.

The Women's Auxiliary was hoping for means to support a lady worker in Loquivy. The women were making a valuable contribution to the witness of the gospel in Paimpol. With two ladies having left and Madame Masclet not able to be as active as usual, there was need for other women workers.

1. Paimpol Archive: copy of *The Friend*, 24 June, 1949; 'Work in Brittany and Paris', *The Pioneer Review*, May 1920.
2. 'A short biographical article on Madame Masclet, 1859-1938', *The Pioneer Review*, January-March, 1939.
3. Paimpol Archive: *The Friend*, 24 June 1949.
4. Ibid., 'Friends' Mission in Brittany'; 'Editorial Forwards', *The Pioneer Review*, May 1921.
5. Jack Hoad, *The Baptists* (Grace Publications, 1986), 164; Sebastian Fath, 'Another Way of Being a Christian in France', from *Baptist History and Heritage*, Winter-Spring, 2001.
6. Pierre Loti based his novel *Pêcheur de Islande* on the fishermen of Paimpol, translated into Welsh by Nathaniel Thomas, *Pysgotwyr Ynys yr Iâ* (1927) and by J. Elwyn Jones, *Pysgotwyr Llydaw* (Denbigh, 1985).
7. Gwyn Griffiths, *Crwydro Llydaw* (Swansea, 1977), 210-1. The rue St Vincent is closed, but Ploubazlanec is mentioned in guide books: information from Michael McGowan, former pastor at Paimpol.
8. Gwyn Griffiths, *Crwydro Llydaw*, 280.
9. Huck, 'Our evangelist and colporteur, Mr Huck', *The Pioneer Review*, July-August 1959. Another colporteur, J. Harry, helped for a brief period, ibid., May 1920.
10. Ibid.
11. Ibid., 'Recent Forward Movement Evangelistic Work in Brittany', May 1921.
12. T. M. Bassett, *The Welsh Baptists and the Missionary Movement*, 61, but does not mention Edgar Jenkins, the son of A. Ll. Jenkins, as one of the workers.
13. 'President's Notes and Comments', *The Pioneer Review*, May 1921.
14. Ibid., 'Recent Forward Movement of Evangelistic Work in Brittany', May 1921; *Knight in Royal Service*, 24.
15. Ibid., 'Paimpol Prospects', May 1921.
16. Ibid., 'Recent Forward Movement Evangelistic Work in Brittany'; *Knight in Royal Service*, 24.
17. Ibid., 'Continental', January-February, 1922/
18. Ibid.
19. Ibid.
20. Ibid., 'All in a week in Paimpol', March-April.

21. Copy of *Cantiques* kindly presented to the author by the church at Paimpol: *Cantiques Evangeliques* (St Brieuc, n.d.).
22. 'Paimpol, Brittany', *The Pioneer Review*, September-October, 1922.
23. Ibid.
24. Ibid.
25. Ibid.
26. Ibid., 'Garden Party at Cardiff', September-October, 1922.
27. Ibid., 'Cardiff Convention', November-December, 1922.
28. Ibi.d, 'Pioneering in the Principality', January-February, 1924.
29. Ibid., 'Cardiff Garden Party', September-October, 1922
30. Ibid., 'President's Notes and Comments', October-December, 1926
31. Ibid., e.g. the Mission benefited from a legacy from Richard Cory, lasting for a period of ten years, and a gift of £100 from the two sisters, 'Miss Cory and Beatrice Cory', in 1925: January-March, 1926.
32. Mrs Richards lived at 23 Longspear Avenue, Cardiff (top of Whitchurch Road), and Mrs Morgan lived in The Mount, near Dr Howells's School.
33. Mr and Mrs Morgan Davies: The grandparents of Mrs Siân Thomas, Pantmawr Road, Cardiff. They were prominent members in Tabernacle Welsh Baptist church, Cardiff. They had a shop, 'Beau March' in Crwys Road, Cardiff.
34. 'Valedictory Service at Cardiff', *The Pioneer Review*, Seprtember-October, 1924. Tabernacle, Cardiff, Sunday school presented her with a French Bible, with signatures of Charles Davies, Pastor, Evan Nicholls, Superintendent and Herbert Phillips, Secretary, dated 8th September 1924: Paimpol Archive.
35. Ibid.
36. Ibid., 'Brittany', September-October, 1924.
37. Ibid., 'Paimpol', April-June, 1925. Scarabin worked with the Wesleyan Mission that had been established in 1904: report on Mission in *Yr Eurgrawn*, April 1919.
38. Ibid., and same report says that 'we had a glorious service, our chapel being almost full to the door, and our people singing Welsh hymn tunes to French words, until the hearts of our Welsh friends were pied into the Hwyl'.
39. Ibid. 'The Holiday Season at Paimpol', October-December, 1926.
40. Ibid., 'Memorable Communion Service', October-December, 1926.
41. Ibid., 'Paimpol', April-June, 1928.
42. Ibid., 'Brittany', January-February, 1924.
43. Ibid.; 'A Short Biographical Article on Madame Masclet, 1859-1938', January-March, 1939.
44. Ibid., 'A Short Biographical Article'.
45. Ibid.
46. Ibid., 'Brittany', January-February, 1924.
47. Ibid. Madame Masclet visited homes regularly, but was prevented from doing so in 1925: 'I have been able to do but little of it, for, after the death of my niece, He has laid on me the charge of three children. These I have

to mother, nurse, teach and lead to the Lord by prayer and the Word of God', ibid. 'Report from Madame Masclet', October-December 1925.

48. Ibid., 'Paimpol', October-December, 1926.
49. Ibid.
50. Ibid. 'Brittany', January-February, 1924.
51. Ibid., 'Paimpol', October-December, 1935.
52. *Knight in Royal Service*, 25.
53. Ibid.
54. 'Brittany', *The Pioneer Review*, July-August, 1922.
55. Ibid.
56. Ibid. 'Our New Missionary for Brittany', May-June, 1924.
57. 'Valedictory Service at Cardiff', September-October, 1924; *Knight in Royal Service*, 33.
58. 'President's Notes and Comments', *The Pioneer Review*, April-June, 1926.
59. Matthews had arrived in Brittany in 1928, and was taking part in meetings during September of that year. Ibid., 'Paimpol', January-March 1929; with photograph of Arthur Matthews, Caradoc Jones and Adolf Huck; *Knight in Royal Service*, 29. Arthur Matthews was born in Roath, Cardiff. His father was a 'Private Traveller', born in Bedminster, Somerset, and the mother was born in Glamorganshire: Census 1901. Arthur Matthews was buried in the cemetery in Kerity.
60. Interview with Edna Evans, né Jones, Ponciau.
61. Ibid.
62. 'My visit to Paimpol', *The Pioneer Review*, October-December, 1928.
63. Ibid.
64. Ibid., 'Paimpol', January-March, 1929
65. Ibid. There had been an earlier work in Lézardrieux, as mentioned in chapter 1.
66. Ibid.
67. Ibid.
68. Ibid.. 'Brittany, our second Mission', January-March, 1929.
69. Ibid.
70. Ibid.
71. Ibid., 'Paimpol;, April-June, 1929.
72. Ibid.
73. Ibid., 'In the villages surrounding Paimpol', April-June, 1929.
74. Ibid., 'Paimpol, a Farewell', October-December, 1929.
75. Ibid.
76. Ibid.
77. Pamphlet, 'The Pioneer Mission Women's Auxiliary', included in Collection, Angus Library.
78. Ibid.

5

PROGRESS IN PAIMPOL
1930-39

Caradoc Jones was always restless; always looking ahead in order
to establish and expand the work. From his early days in Paimpol he
desired a motor car so that he could travel the country. That desire
was fulfilled in 1926. He believed that it was essential for the witness
of the gospel to have a building near the centre of the town. Land
had been purchased in 1926, but the building had not been erected.
Furthermore Caradoc Jones was deeply concerned with the plight of
orphan children in Paimpol and the surrounding area. He had
already helped with three orphans that had been placed in a French
Orphanage.[1] He would not be satisfied until the church or temple, as
they would say in Paimpol, and the orphanage, were erected.

THE NEW CHAPEL
Definite steps were taken to build the chapel during 1929 and it was
possible to begin building in 1930. Dr McCaig and Charles Phillips
of the Pioneer Mission attended the laying of the foundation.[2]
Caradoc Jones met them at St Brieuc, and at Paimpol they were
welcomed by the Welsh contingent from Cardiff. Dr McCaig
preached on the Sunday before the ceremony. There was also a
Communion service and greetings from Wales. During the day, six
people applied for baptism.

At 3 o'clock, Whitmonday, a good crowd gathered for the laying
of the foundation. There were representatives from Wales, England,
and many places in Brittany including St Brieuc, Morlaix and

Tremel. Dr McCaig laid the first stone and also brought a gift of £50 from friends. Morgan Davies, Cardiff, laid two stones, one in memory of the deceased Evan Nicholls, Cardiff, and the other in his own name. He also gave a gift of £25 for each stone. Caradoc Jones laid the fourth stone and tea followed after the meeting, kindly provided by Mrs Morgan Davies, Cardiff. Other gifts from friends were received during the day.[3]

Through the medium of the *Pioneer Review*, Caradoc Jones invited friends to the opening of the new chapel. They could combine the visit with a holiday in Brittany. Ten or twelve pounds would cover the cost of a ten-day holiday, travelling from Southampton to St. Malo. Twelve to fourteen pounds would cover the same period, travelling through Paris. It is not known how many people responded to his invitation, but it is known that a large crowd gathered for the opening of the new chapel.[4]

On Sunday, 31 August 1930, the old chapel was used for public worship for the last time, when the preachers for the morning, afternoon and evening were Pastor Oriol, Paris, fellow student with Caradoc Jones at Spurgeon's College, Charles Phillips of the Pioneer Mission and Pastor Daulle, Brest. It was during the afternoon meeting that Arthur Matthews was set apart to minister in Paimpol and the surrounding areas. He already had two years' experience of different kind of ministries and Caradoc Jones must have been glad that his fellow worker from Cardiff was settling down so well.[5]

The new building was opened on Monday, 1 September 1930, made to accommodate about a hundred people. It could not contain all those that flocked to Paimpol on this special occasion. A great variety of fashion was evident: the latest Parisian, London, Cardiff fashion and 'the beautiful, homely Breton fashion with their variety of coiffes'.[6] In a predominantly Roman Catholic country, it must have been a great joy for Caradoc Jones to see so many Protestant denominations being represented: Baptist, Wesleyan, Reformed and Welsh Calvinistic Methodist. The representative of the Welsh

Calvinistic Methodist was Gerlan Williams, a missionary who had worked in India as well as in Brittany. He was continuing the work in Quimper that the denomination had established in 1844. The first Calvinistic Methodist missionary in Brittany preached his first sermon in French, in Morlaix, where, a few years earlier, the Baptists had established a cause.[7]

The countries France, England and Wales were represented. Caradoc Jones referred, not only to Wales, but specifically to Cardiff: 'But, and this is surely pardonable, our hearts waxed warmer and warmer as we saw and communed with our Cardiff friends, who have been such valiant supporters of the Paimpol Mission since its commencement'. [8] The pastor also rejoiced at the presence of two persons from north Wales, one of them being his nephew.[9]

Mrs Cornelius Griffiths, from Cardiff, opened the new building. She, and her husband, were keen supporters of the work in Paimpol, and an engraved stone was placed on the right hand side leading to the chapel in memory of her husband. In the chapel, Pastor Oriol, Paris, offered the dedication prayer and preached from 1 Peter 1:16: 'Because it is written, Be ye holy for I am holy'. Two meetings were held after lunch. Dr McCaig, London; Pastor Somerville, Tremel; and Charles Phillips, Pioneer Mission, spoke in the first meeting. The speakers in the other meeting were Rev. Gerlan Williams, Quimper; Rev. Benignius, Lorient; and 'by special request' Pastor Oriol, Paris.[10]

During the series of meetings, Morgan Davies brought greetings from Cardiff and addressed the congregation briefly. He made a number of contrasts. He contrasted the Protestant and Roman Catholic Faith, and the prophetic and sacramental ministry. He expressed the hope that soon Brittany would be training her own pastors. As an encouragement to the church at Paimpol, he advised them not to despise the day of small things. Paul only had a few humble women in Philippi, but in a short time the gospel spread through the whole of Europe.[11] At the end of the series of meetings, all enjoyed a tea together, the expenses being covered by Mrs Pullen of Cardiff. The following day, Tuesday, the Protestant churches in Brittany met in Paimpol, representing five denominations. Mrs Cornelius Griffiths provided the tea on that occasion.[12]

By September 1930, the Protestants in Paimpol had a chapel, hall and manse, all under the same roof. The pastor also had a garage to keep his car. Caradoc Jones and his fellow worshippers were highly delighted with the new building: 'The chapel is a fine, substantial structure built of stone, with granite facings, and being in an elevated state, has quite a commanding appearance. The back part of the building comprises the manse, after the continental fashion'.[13] At the apex, over the entrance, a hand holding the cross was portrayed with the words (in Latin) 'I both hold and am held', being the motto of Spurgeon's College. On the walls a number of Scripture texts had been written in French and 'A notable feature of the chapel is the marble baptistry, which will be a constant testimony to the Truth for which we stand'.[14]

During the meetings to open the chapel a number of people professed conversion. Two Sundays later, two of them, two women, were baptized on the basis of their faith in Christ. A large, curious crowd witnessed the baptism because it was held when the people from the Roman Catholic Church were coming from Mass. They followed the congregation from the church to the seaside where the baptism was to take place. The two candidates gave a word of testimony, Mr Matthews prayed and the two were baptized to the singing of the doxology.[15]

When Charles Phillips visited Paimpol in 1931, he was delighted that he could stay in the Manse and was much encouraged by the work of the church. He preached on the Sunday and then gave two lantern lectures, one on 'Palestine' and the other on the 'Life of Christ'. He believed that the text on the board outside the church was an effective means of evangelism, especially as it was illuminated at night. There were no streetlights, therefore the text was most striking.[16]

The members and their pastor wondered what the response to the new chapel might be in Paimpol. They ventured out to invite people to attend. Madame Huck met a few people on the street and some of them promised to attend a service. They kept their word and attended the chapel. The pastor himself, writing nine months after the opening of the church could say that 'Hardly has one Sunday passed since the opening day that some strangers have turned in to see the church, admire it, and often to join with us in the whole service'. [17] When the new building was erected a new chapter in the Protestant work in Paimpol was opened. The next step was to give attention to the need for an orphanage.

THE ORPHANAGE

When the worshippers moved to the new building, the obvious question was 'What should be done with the old chapel?' There were a number of possibilities. It could be sold; it could be turned into a private house or it could be used as an orphanage. There was general agreement that this was the opportunity to have an orphanage.[18]

In deciding to open an orphanage, the Paimpol church was governed by three motives. One was a Christian humanitarian concern for orphans, those who needed comfort, love, food and clothing. Secondly, there was a religious and anti-Catholic motive. The Paimpol church was conscious of the influence that the priests had on the children. The other motive was evangelical, the desire to see children under their care coming to faith in the Lord Jesus Christ.

The venture was a demanding one. The building had to be divided into rooms to accommodate eight beds. There was a need for a kitchen, dining room and toilets. It was necessary to dig a well in order to have sufficient clean water. The estimated cost was £300. As he had done before, Charles Phillips promised to help financially and his kind gesture fed the optimism of the church. Workers were forthcoming. Miss Mary Cave, who had worked on a voluntary basis with the Baptists at Morlaix for eight years, volunteered to be responsible for the orphanage. She was also willing to furnish half of the place, meet the cost of a large part of the expenses and was also ready to help in feeding the children. A Breton friend of hers, Mademoiselle Ropars, was happy to join as a helper. A retired schoolteacher knew of the need for a teacher, and immediately and willingly offered her services.[19]

All of those involved in the work looked forward eagerly to the opening of the orphanage, 24 September 1931. Friends from the orphanage at Tremel, and friends from St. Brieuc joined the members of the church at Paimpol. First of all a service was held outside the building, before going in to see the inside. In that service, Arthur Matthews, Adolph Huck and Terrell, who was in Paimpol at the time, took part. Miss Phillips spoke briefly and Terrell handed her the key to open the door of the orphanage. The crowd, including the orphans that had been accepted, rushed into the building, anxious to see how it had been transformed. The company then moved to the schoolroom of the new chapel to enjoy a splendid tea. A collection during the day realized £66-10-0.[20]

Five children were received into the orphanage: Henry, a tomboy; Yvette, his sister; Gene, an orphan from Paris; Yves, 'an enterprising boy of three', and Lili, the baby of the family, who was prone to break everything within reach.[21] Two other children were received into the home at the beginning of 1932.[22] They were Claude and Albert. Claude had lost his mother and the father was ill with consumption. The little one was used to going to Mass and would sing 'Ave Maria', but now he was taught to sing 'Ave Jesus'. Albert was 'a lovely black haired, black-eyed boy of fifteen months'. He could strut around and his favourite hobby was hiding the shoes of the other children. Albert's father was suffering from mental illness and the mother had to work making it impossible for her to look after the baby.[23]

It was also possible to receive the elderly Madame Noel and elderly Madame Le Treize, who was seventy-eight years of age. She had suffered much because of her faith and this was also true of her late husband. They sacrificed greatly for the sake of their son's education, but he disowned them because they were Protestants. Caradoc Jones had lodged with them for five years during the early years of his ministry. The pastor paid tribute to her by saying that her spiritual life was becoming stronger as her physical life was becoming weaker. It was most appropriate that the church was now giving one of them a home.[24]

Miss Cave sent a report to the Council, early 1932:[25]

> Since Christmas our little Home has been invaded by sickness. With rains and mists of January there came to the little town of Paimpol four diseases – influenza, croup, mumps and measles – and our little ones were not exempt. All but Yves, the scapegrace of the family, were attacked by two or three of these maladies. Owing to the goodness of the Lord, no serious complications arose, and now our little band is about again, none the worse for the two or three weeks in bed.

Such a difficulty as illness had to be faced and the children could be troublesome but in spite of everything, the little ones were a source of great joy for the carers and the church.

THE STORY OF AMEDINE

A number of stories could be related concerning the orphanage. The one that stands out is the story of Amedine.[26] The mother died when Amedine was very young, and she was only fifteen years of age when Caradoc Jones first met her. By that time she was a slave in the home of a drunken father and uncaring brothers and sisters. To make matters worse the father brought another woman to live in the home. Amedine suffered physically because of her father's brutality. It is not known why she came to one of the meetings in the church at Paimpol, but in the very first service that she attended, Amedine responded to the call of the gospel and was converted. The fruit of the work of grace was soon evident in her life.[27]

Amedine's father was furious when he realized that his daughter had been converted. On one occasion he chased his daughter with a knife: 'She ran and climbed up to the hayloft. He followed and when near enough, threw the knife at her as she stood against the wall, just like Saul with David. She dodged successfully and made a dash for the ladder down which she sped to safety'.[28] She found herself in an impossible situation and decided to escape from home. The move further infuriated the father and he went around looking for his daughter, again threatening to kill her.[29] Caradoc Jones, and others from the church, were alarmed and informed the police of the father's threats. Amedine continued to attend meetings and started taking part in prayer. She would pray for two things, her father's conversion and for revival in Brittany. The prayer for her father was a sure sign of grace as was the prayer for revival. That latter aspect also says something of Caradoc Jones. He was continually reminding the church for the need of revival. Amedine applied for baptism, knowing very well that this would enrage her father and increase the danger to her life.[30]

Caradoc Jones arranged for Amedine to live in a Christian home. The father continued to hunt her and one morning arrived at the Manse, hardly able to control himself with anger. The pastor was able to calm him and sent him home, rebuking him for behaving so shamefully. He urged him to behave as a responsible father.[31]

The father was taken ill. In the love of the gospel, the young girl ventured home, anxious to look after him. Slowly, she was accepted and the father's attitude changed completely. He even asked his daughter to arrange for the pastor to call. Caradoc Jones responded willingly and shared the gospel with the needy man, who listened intently to the good news of salvation in Christ. Caradoc Jones prayed and then asked Amedine to do so:[32]

She knelt at his bed and began to pray. And she COULD pray. I have seldom heard a girl pray like it. I could hardly hold back the tears to hear this girl pray for a father who had sought her life, and was now neglected by the rest of the family. But the effect on the father was overwhelming. He wept and wept until the bed shook. She rose from her knees knowing now that her father was in the safe keeping of 'The Friend of Sinners'. Bending over the dying one, she took his hand and kissed him saying that she would come again to see him and she did until the call came.

Caradoc Jones witnessed the triumph of grace over flesh and blood and possibly the triumph over satanic opposition.

Even after her father's death, life was difficult for Amedine.[33] She was left to work on a farm and the attitude of her brothers and sisters did not change. They were still antagonistic and sent one brother, Maurice, to a Roman Catholic school. Amedine continued to attend the meetings and one thing she could do for Maurice was take him with her to the services. Another expression of her zeal was the fifty francs gift that she gave to the church. She was in service and must have sacrificed to be able to give such a sum. Amedine returned home for a while to care for her sister, Madelaine, and her brother Maurice.[34] Eventually it was possible for Madelaine and Maurice to have a place in the orphanage. Through the sister's witness and the attendance at the services, both Madelaine and Maurice were converted and baptized on profession of their faith in the Lord Jesus Christ. Time came for Maurice to leave the orphanage but Madelaine made it possible for him to stay. She offered her services as a servant for the keep of her brother. Amedine returned to service in order to earn her living. [35]

The story reveals what a simple but strong faith in Christ can accomplish and that in a young girl in her teens. The orphanage was fulfilling its aims. Madelaine, Maurice and the other children were cared for physically, Maurice had been taken from a Roman Catholic school and the brother and sister were the first fruits of the gospel in the orphanage.

PAIMPOL AND SURROUNDING DISTRICTS

Caradoc Jones concentrated on the work in Paimpol but he cast his keen eye over other areas as well. He reported on the happy time they had during Christmas 1931 in St Barbe, St Rion and Kerlouri.[36] The pastor also worked in close conjunction with other workers. He was always glad to have a lady working with him in the church at Paimpol. Not only could she work among the members she could also visit the women in the area. One of the zealous witnesses was Mademoiselle Deleu. After finishing her course at Nogent sur Marne, she served as a deaconess in the church at Paimpol, while waiting for an opening to go to the Ivory Coast. When she left, Mademoiselle Coquin followed her in the church. When she was appointed it was suggested that a suitable uniform should be found for her. A gift was received for that purpose from the Women's Auxiliary and she had her uniform.[37]

Mademoiselle Coquin helped with the work in the village of Loquivy. A house was found that was to be the centre of the Protestant work. Caradoc Jones joined her for the first meeting at that place. He related what happened on his arrival: 'Arriving at the village at 7.30, we found almost all the houses in darkness and shuttered up. We could hardly count the houses in all the village where there was light'.[38] He found only Mademoiselle Coquin and a little girl present. They decided to go outside and walk through the streets calling 'Reunion, Reunion'. They passed the place where they had held open-air services, but there was only one man there lurking in the darkness. He was asked why the place was in darkness and replied that:[39]

Some of the men had gone off to the coasts of England to fish in English waters, and that they had been away three days. The others had gone out that evening, and that explained why there were no men there. As for the women they have gone to bed, and even if they had not, it is questionable if they would have come to the meeting, for this is the village from which two evangelists have been chased on two occasions by the women, who are a very bigoted lot.

Returning to their centre, the three of them, Caradoc Jones, Mademoiselle Coquin and the little girl sang and prayed. As they were leaving they saw three young men in the yard and invited them back for a meeting. They agreed and a brief service was held.

Unperturbed, the witnesses returned to the village the following week. By this time the men had returned home. When missionaries arrived they could see that a travelling cinema had been set up opposite their place of meeting. As on the previous occasion, they went around crying 'Reunion, Reunion'. The cinema people responded by shouting that it was their 'Reunion' at 8 o'clock. Ten men, however, agreed to come to the service for half an hour and then leave to go to the cinema. When it was time to start the meeting, twenty people were present. Soon the cinema band of kettledrums began to play loudly, but the congregation remained and declared that 'This is our cinema tonight'.[40] They stayed to the end of the service.

The other workers, Colporteur Huck and his wife, were plodders, and travelled the country distributing tracts and Scriptures. Madame Huck mentioned how she met with different kinds of people. During one afternoon she met a·person who was very antagonistic to the gospel and she soon realized that he was a Bolshevist. In the market she met a lady and her daughter who were keeping a lodging house, with whom she had a profitable discussion. Later, they attended a meeting in the church. Another lady expressed a desire for a Bible as she had been without one for some time, that is, since a Roman Catholic priest had taken it from her.[41]

The son of Colporteur Huck and his wife, a member in the church at Paimpol, was installing electricity in a house, about eight miles from the town.[42] As he worked he was whistling a hymn tune and the lady of the house recognized it and was glad to find that he was a Protestant. She had attended a Baptist church in Paris but, out of a family of six, only the lady and her mother were Protestants. The son informed his father of the visit and he lost no time before visiting the home. He visited them on a number of occasions and another two of the family showed real interest in the gospel. Even during the first visit, the family was happy to have a hymn sung and for the colporteur to offer prayer. Before leaving on that occasion, he sold a Bible to the family, and when he returned later, found out that those interested in spiritual matters had been reading the Scriptures regularly.[43]

The family was invited to services in the church at Paimpol. They attended the Christmas services and a baptismal service that deeply touched them. On another occasion they attended a Communion service, when they sat at the back with non-members. As a result of these visits the work of grace was becoming evident in the lives of some of the family. Another visit to the home confirmed this judgement.[44]

The Bible divided the people of Brittany. In the Protestant churches the exposition of the Word of God was central, while in the Roman Catholic churches the liturgical and sacramental aspects were central. Most, if not all of the Protestant homes would have a Bible, while most Roman Catholic homes did not have one. The Protestant leaders would encourage the people to read it, but the priests would discourage the people from doing so. It was a great encouragement for Caradoc Jones, and the other leaders, to learn that members were defying the priest when he would tell them not to read the Scriptures. One widow made her stand in an unusual way. She had an open Bible sculptured on her late husband's gravestone, with the words: 'He that believeth on Me, though he were dead, yet shall he live'.[45] It was difficult to introduce a Bible culture into a country dominated by a Church culture for many centuries, because it involved a radical change, personally and socially.

Mademoiselle Coquin was giving all of her time to work with Caradoc Jones. She arranged a Bible school for children at Paimpol on Thursday evenings. She did some work in outlying villages but visited one particular place every Wednesday night. During the holiday period a number of children from Paris came for a holiday and stayed for several weeks. It was an opportunity to meet them regularly and to come to know them quite well. [46] Arthur Matthews, Caradoc Jones' co-worker, married Mlle. Coquin and they concentrated on St Quay and Plouha, where they had a room that held about forty people. Consequently, Caradoc Jones had to shoulder more responsibility.[47]

The extra responsibilities did not prevent the pastor from visiting a number of different villages. [48] Apart from the outstations, he kept in touch with the Baptist work in Brittany. For example, children from the orphanage and members of the church visited Plougrescant, some eighteen miles from Paimpol. They had a glorious day at the outstation of the Baptist Missionary Society. They had a picnic together and the intention was to have an evening service. That was postponed because it was the time for wheat threshing and it would be very difficult for many people to attend. They did look forward to a meeting at a more convenient time.[49]

It was arranged for a group from Paimpol to visit Plougrescant during November 1935. It consisted of Caradoc Jones, Mr and Mrs Matthews, colporteur Huck, Mr Chapallez, Miss Cave and Miss Edna Jones. During the day it poured with rain and one of the group was soaked to the skin. He had to borrow a suit of clothes in order to attend the meeting. It was too small for the person, causing Caradoc Jones to comment that 'borrowed plumes are not always the best'.[50] The rain had made it difficult for many to travel, but there was a good congregation when the service commenced. Latecomers arrived and it was necessary to find extra chairs and benches. The Paimpol people were pleased with the devotional spirit of the meeting and all present enjoyed the singing. The place was also full for the second meeting, when three Paimpol church members gave their personal testimony.[51]

The rain and the roads are reminders of some of the difficulties of working in Brittany. It was an advantage to have a bicycle, but even that means of transport was not a great help in stormy weather. A car could be a great help on some roads, but the workers were afraid to drive at any time on some of the narrower roads in Brittany.[52] There were social considerations to be taken into account. Reference has been made to the men going away for days and sometimes weeks. Men reaching the age of eighteen were called up for national service. Many young men and women could not find work and left for other towns and cities, including Paris, in exactly the same way the youngsters of Wales would leave for Liverpool and London.[53] Many of those that did not go away would indulge in cider drinking. The church persevered, believing that it had a divine mission in Brittany.

CONTINUING ENCOURAGEMENT

In spite of uncertainties and opposition, the missionaries acknowledged that there were many positive aspects to their mission. It was possible to arrange other baptismal services; support was still coming from Wales and a number of places in England, and a few new workers joined the church.

Baptism was regarded as an act of obedience to the Lord Jesus Christ, but it was also a public confession of faith in Christ. The convert would make it clear that he was taking his stand for the Saviour and identifying himself with the church at Paimpol,

101

whatever the consequences might be. There were a few of outstanding events during the thirties. On one particular Sunday three other persons were baptized:[54]

> Yet another cause of rejoicing, and a heartening one for us, was to see a few Sundays ago, three witnessing for their Lord in baptism. One, a woman of seventy-five, and who had a torture of a time to break away from the shackles of Rome; the other a young widow about thirty-five, who also had much to contend with on account of her new found faith; and a young girl of fifteen, who had fled a fearful home, and was converted on hearing the gospel the first time.

During the service five more people responded to the invitation to be baptized. The reference to the fifteen year old must be a reference to Amedine. Her sister Madaline and her brother Maurice were also baptized.

Caradoc Jones was in contact with the mother and two daughters in the Baudic Lighthouse.[55] They were Protestants but had not been baptized as believers. They became convinced of the Scriptural basis for such a baptism and were baptized in the church at Paimpol. On one Sunday in 1934, two candidates were baptized. On another Sunday five were baptized. Among the candidates were a lady who had attended services for some time; two lads from St Barbe, one of them being the son of Huck, the colporteur and the son of the first convert at St Barbe. During the service, others responded to the call to be baptized.[56] After a period without any candidates, the church rejoiced when three people applied for baptism, a lady of nearly sixty, a young lad from the orphanage and a young lady.[57]

Persevering in Brittany would have been much harder but for the support from outside. Support continued to come from Wales, especially from Cardiff, and Garden Parties were still being held.[58] Caradoc Jones made an effort to be present at the Garden Parties as often as possible. He was present for the 1931 event. He spoke eloquently of the need in Brittany and appealed for help.[59] Morgan Davies and his wife were still zealous for the cause and they also arranged Garden Parties. The Cardiff supporters did not forget the importance of prayer and came together to intercede for the success of the gospel in Brittany. During 1935 a formal resolution was proposed that 'we all present do pledge ourselves to do all in our power by prayer and practical sympathy to support the Paimpol Mission'. A note was added to that report, 'Except for this Cardiff effort, the work in Brittany could not have been carried on at all – certainly not to the extent as has been possible'.[60]

Whenever possible, Caradoc Jones visited Wales and occasionally toured England and Scotland on behalf of the Pioneer Mission. Two of the supporting churches in England were Slough and Langley Baptist churches. Not only did Caradoc Jones visit them they also visited Paimpol. A group of fourteen, led by J. J. Hull, visited Paimpol during the summer of 1937. They made a valuable contribution to the work. They taught the children and played with them and took part in meetings in the church. Some of them visited Ste Barbe, where two of them spoke; one sang a solo and one played the organ. The leader of the group spoke in French in the open-air meetings. This was an added bonus.[61]

The church at Paimpol was always ready to take advantage of the holiday period, especially during the summer. A fortnight's holiday was allowed with pay and this meant that a large number of visitors arrived in Paimpol. The summer of 1937 was a glorious one, weather wise, and Paimpol and other coastal towns were crowded with visitors.[62] The church launched an open-air campaign in towns and villages, in fairs and markets. They mapped out the area comprising of different places within about twenty miles of Paimpol. The church was glad that the voluntary offerings had increased which was a great help to cover extra costs. Nearly fifteen places were visited, some of them quite often. For example, the witnesses visited Treguier markets and fairs eight times; Loquivy, six times, and five extra meetings were held in Paimpol itself. All this activity was in addition to the usual work of the church in Paimpol and the stations.[63]

New workers were always welcomed. A few arrived during 1937 and 1938. Miss Nellie Jones had worked in Belgium for a while and was a French speaker.[64] After returning from Belgium she trained at Hermon Bible College. She arrived in Brittany having covered the first part of the journey at the speed of eighty miles an hour and the last twenty-five miles to Paimpol at the crawling rate of eight miles an hour. On the second Sunday after her arrival she was set apart for her task. For a fortnight she had to take care of the orphanage while Miss Cave was having a much-needed rest. Nellie Jones also visited many villages and concentrated on Bourg of L. There had been some Protestant work there about thirty years earlier, and some of the people remembered some of the hymns that were sung in the services. Her main problem was to find a room or a hall to hold meetings. At the end of her first year in Paimpol she was still looking for a suitable place.[65]

Nellie Jones started on her work alone, but soon Mademoiselle Ndelec joined her. [66] She was a converted Roman Catholic. After her conversion she was taken ill and during that time came to know a Christian friend with whom she shared her desire to go to Bible College. The friend gave her information concerning Nogent sur Marne, Paris. She trained at the College and a door of service opened for her at Paimpol. As she settled down she had three classes of people in mind, apart from the practicing Roman Catholics, 1. The ignorant who knew nothing of the word of God. 2. Those who had heard the gospel recently or in the past. She was anxious to have a room where she could meet with such people. 3. Those indifferent to every aspect of religion, including atheists and freethinker. The two women were glad of the opportunity to work together.[67]

Arthur Matthews was optimistic concerning the work at Plouha. This was evident in his report for 1935: 'For progress made during the year we have to thank God, and take courage for the future'.[68] More people were attending the service, including a family consisting of parents and nine children. Arthur Matthews was thrilled that the lady who opened her home for worship was standing strong in the faith. In Lanvollon, a place like Plouha of about 1,500 population, many were ready to listen to the gospel and one person had been reading and re-reading the Gospels. At the end of 1937, Arthur Matthews was most grateful for what had been accomplished. Many had responded to conversations and generally the people were more ready to accept tracts and Scriptures. Even house-to-house witness was not so difficult. Another source of amazement was the faithfulness of the aged people.[69]

Difficulties at the orphanage had been overcome to some extent, but there was a terrible lack of space. Fortunately, a small house opposite the orphanage was secured and provided an extra dormitory and a storeroom, but there was still need for room to expand. Madelaine was still there, working as payment for her brother Maurice's board. One of the orphans had been apprenticed to an engineer and Maurice was preparing for his Brevet. On the one hand, the carers at the Orphanage rejoiced because of progress but on the other hand were worried because of the lack of space.[70]

By 1939, the work at St Barbe and Plouha was strengthened and especially at Paimpol. Significant beginnings had been made in many other places. Those who laboured in the different places were still persevering and a few new missionaries had joined the Mission. Caradoc Jones himself had gained the sympathy of a large number of people, not only in Paimpol, but in surrounding areas as well. The number of converts in a Roman Catholic country was most encouraging. A church, manse and hall had been built at a cost of £3,000. The orphanage was under the care of a devoted lady. In 1939 eight workers, including Women's Auxiliary Workers, were bearing witness to the gospel in Paimpol and neighbouring villages.[71] It is true that the church was still facing a number of difficulties, but steady progress had been made. The missionaries sacrificed, but knew that they had to continue by faith. Little did they realize that greater difficulties lay ahead and that greater sacrifices would be demanded from them. Before the end of 1939 France was involved in a World War. In different ways all the members and missionaries in Paimpol, and other districts, would be involved in the horrendous events of the period from 1939 to 1945.

1. *Knight in Royal Service*, 29.
2. 'Paimpol Re-visited', *The Pioneer Review'*, July-September, 1930.
3. Ibid.
4. Ibid., 'The price of progress'.
5. *Knight in Royal Service*, 29; Gerlan Williams, 'Capel Newydd yn Llydaw', *Y Cenhadwr*, November 1930.
6. Charles Phillips, 'Description of Paimpol Chapel and Manse', *The Pioneer Review*, October-December, 1930.
7. Ibid.
8. Ibid.
9. Ibid.
10. Ibid.
11. Information received from Mrs Siân Thomas, Cardiff, grand -daughter of Mr and Mrs Morgan Davies.
12. 'Our Church', *The Pioneer Review*, October-December, 1930; *Knight in Royal Service*, 31.
13. Ibid., 'Paimpol Revisited', July-September, 1930
14. Ibid., 'Description of Paimpol Chapel and Manse', October-December, 1930.
15. Ibid., 'Our New Church'.
16. Ibid., 'Visit to Paimpol by Mr. Charles Phillips', April-June, 1931.
17. Ibid., 'Paimpol: Cause for rejoicing', July-September, 1931
18. *Knight in Royal Service*, 32.
19. 'The Opening of a Children's Home', *The Pioneer Review*, October-December 1931.
20. Ibid.
21. Ibid., The Chidren's Home', January-March, 1932.
22. Ibid., April-June, 1932.
23. Ibid.
24. Ibid., 'Paimpol', January-March, 1932; ; ibid., January-March 1933.
25. Ibid., 'Paimpol', April-June, 1932.
26. Ibid. 'Paimpol': 'The Story of Amedine', January-March, 1932.
27. Ibid.
28. Angus Library: typed account of the story, 'Her Sad Face'.
29. Ibid.

30. 'Paimpol', *The Pioneer Review*, January-March, 1932.
31. 'Her Sad Face'.
32. Ibid.
33. Paimpol', *The Pioneer Review*, April-June, 1932.
34. Ibid.
35. Ibid., 'Triumphs of Grace from the Orphanage', April-June, 1935.
36. Ibid., 'Paimpol', January-March, 1932.
37. Ibid., 'Concerning the Women's Auxiliary', April-June, 1931; ibid. July-September, 1931.
38. Ibid., 'Paimpol', April-June, 1932.
39. Ibid.
40. Ibid.
41. Ibid., 'Report from Madame Huck', April-June, 1931.
42. Ibid., 'Problems and Progress at Paimpol', July-September, 1935.
43. Ibid.
44. Ibid.
45. Ibid., 'Paimpol-Bibles to the Front', April-June, 1931.
46. Ibid., 'Concerning the Women's Auxiliary', July-September, 1931.
47. *Knight in Royal Service*, 34.
48. 'Brittany', *The Pioneer Review*, January-March, 1936.
49. Ibid.
50. Ibid.
51. Ibid.
52. *Knight in Royal Service*, 34.
53. 'Problems and Progress in Paimpol', *The Pioneer Review*, July-September, 1935.
54. Ibid., 'Cause for rejoicing', July September, 1931.
55. Ibid. 'Paimpol', January-March, 1932.
56. Ibid., 'Brittany', January-March, 1935.
57. Ibid., 'Paimpol. Summer Activity', 0ctober-November, 1937.
58. It was a great loss to lose Mrs Richards, a faithful Cardiff supporter, but her place was taken by Miss O. Edwards, Ibid., 'Paimpol', July-September, 1931; 'Cardiff Garden Party', July-September 1932. Garden Parties: e.g. July-September, 1932, July-September, 1935.
59. Ibid., 'Paimpol', October-December, 1931.
60. Ibid., 'The Cardiff Garden Party', July-September, 1935.
61. Ibid., 'Our Holiday in Brittany', 0ctober-November, 1937. Supporting churches in the London area included Chatsworth Road, Norwood; Woodside, south Norwood and Muswell Hill, where Melville Evans ministered; he moved to Porthcawl, south Wales and continued a staunch supporter of the Pioneer Mission.
62. Ibid., 'We have seen in our Church more visitors this year than ever, in spite of the indifference of the masses to religion', 'Paimpol. Summer Activity'.
63. Ibid.
64. Ibid., 'Miss Nellie Jones', January-March, 1938.

65. Ibid., 'A message from our worker Mlle Ndelec', January-March, 1939.
66. Ibid.
67. Ibid.
68. 'A letter from Mr Matthews', January–March, 1935.
69. Ibid., 'Plouha', January-March, 1938.
70. Ibid., 'The Children's Home', January-March, 1939.
71. *The Pioneer Mission Jubilee, 1889-1939.*

6

PAIMPOL AND BESANÇON
1939-40

Before the end of 1939, war was ravaging most of Europe. Caradoc Jones was a British citizen in France, an enemy of Germany. He knew very well what could happen if Germany conquered France.

THE WAR

On 1 September 1939, Germany invaded Poland, an event that, two days later, led to a declaration of war by Britain and France on Germany.[1] Both France and Britain had strong military forces, and Britain had an able leader in Winston Churchill.[2] France also had a strong army. There was no doubt that 'On paper, the French army looked at least a match for the Germans'.[3] It was Germany, however, that gained victory during the early part of the war. The German army marched from Poland through the Low Countries on 10 May 1940, and the Allied Forces (Britain and France) were forced to retreat to Dunkirk. Three hundred thousand troops were confined within one area of seven miles. It was a hopeless situation, as they had the sea behind them and the Germans in front. About 860 vessels of all kinds took part in an amazing rescue operation.[4] They even included 372 small crafts, of which 170 were sunk. Over three hundred thousand troops were. rescued, thousands died and thousands were taken prisoners.[5]

In spite of German advances, Churchill in Britain and Reynaud, the French Prime Minister, were still optimistic concerning the war. They even discussed a Declaration of Union between Britain and

France. Reynaud was enthusiastic. The French Cabinet did not share the Prime Minister's optimism and acknowledged, that shortly France would have to surrender. Germany's position was strengthened when Italy came to her aid on 10 June 1940. Winston Churchill had a meeting with Reynaud, General de Gaulle and others on 16 June 1940 and the British Prime Minister reported that

> Presently, when we left the dinner table and sat with some coffee and brandy, M. Reynaud told me that Marshall Petain had informed him that it would be necessary for France to seek an armistice.[6]

The French leaders were divided, and also failed to realize where the Allies would attack. The Germans were able to march to Paris before the end of May 1940. They entered the city on 14 June. On 22nd of the month a surrender treaty was signed: 'France lay prostrate, beaten in a 42 day campaign that stunned the world'.[7]

A message went out from the German headquarters that flags were to be flown and church bells to ring: The order was read on the German wireless. Three minutes' silence followed, and then came the playing of 'The March into Paris', specially composed for the occasion. One correspondent reported that:[8]

> It was a strangely empty Paris that awaited the arrival of the Germans. Only a few police were seen on the streets. A handful of soldiers and some civilians wandered about aimlessly. Some housewives were doing their shopping at the only baker's shop still open in the West End. A mobile guard was posted at the door of the shop, a gun slung over his shoulder.

Another author describes the roads jammed with cars, wagons and horses carrying trunks and furniture. The people were rushing along, 'The people are half mad, they don't even reply to what we ask them'.[9] What could be seen were:[10]

Dead horses along the side of the road; cows lowing in pain because they had not been milked for days; abandoned birdcages; stray cats and dogs.

The humiliation was complete.

The same author gave the title 'The Exodus' to one of his chapters. Millions of people left their homes. Many left before there was real danger, while others had to leave hurriedly while having a meal. The people in Paris and other parts of France were leaving their homes and refugees from Belgium poured into the country. Very often they arrived in villages that had already been vacated by the French and there would be nothing at all left there. The events that led to the capture of Paris turned 'a mere military defeat to something approaching the disintegration of an entire society'.[11] The humiliation created a deep hatred of the enemy in the French people.

As the result of the surrender of Paris, France was divided into two; the occupied territory to the north, where Paimpol was located and unoccupied territory to the south, governed from Vichy.[12] France had to pay occupation costs; French prisoners were to remain in captivity and Jews in France handed over to the Germans. Although unoccupied, until 1942, the Vichy Government collaborated with Germany and carried out her policies.

The Jews especially suffered from their own Government: 'On 22 July 1940, Vichy created a naturalization revision committee to study the cases of some 500,000 cases of immigrants naturalized since 1927: 15,000 were stripped of their citizenship, 40 per cent of whom were Jews'.[13] In a few months time the Jews were excluded from all the public services.

In 1942 the whole of France was occupied, but that made no difference at all to the Vichy authorities. They continued to collaborate with Germany. In doing so they knew that their lives were safe and that they would benefit personally. Vichy was supposed to work for the benefit of national interests, but 'In

111

practice, it was a hotbed of political intrigue providing ample scope for old third Republic hands such as Pierre Laval and Flandin to exercise their talents for backstairs manipulation'.[14] They were, really, puppets of Germany.

PAIMPOL, 1939-40

As in other countries, the war created a gap among the people of Brittany, because the able bodied men were called to military service. The children, mothers and the older people were left at home. Paimpol felt the loss of many men, but a few workers that had retired renewed their service, which was a great help in such a trying time. In the early days of the war it was still possible to hold open-air meetings and distribute tracts.[15] Arthur Matthews was persevering in Plouha, and there, as in Paimpol the women had to accept more responsibility than usual.[16]

Paimpol experienced losses and gains. The church lost two workers when Miss N. Jones and Mademoiselle Ndelec left,[17] but there was an increase in numbers when evacuees from other parts of France arrived. They did not stay long, however, because they were taken to some of the large towns. During 1939-40, some soldiers started attending the services, including one pastor, referred to as a 'very lively witness'.[18] He moved to another camp twenty miles away, making it difficult for him to attend the services. He was so keen that on a few occasions he attempted hitchhiking to church, perhaps not the wisest thing to do during a time of war.[19]

Other aspects of the work encouraged the church. When the workers were out distributing tracts they met a lady who was very ready to talk concerning her spiritual need. She had married when she was twenty-two and went to the priest for confession. The lady was so disgusted with the priest's response she determined to find a 'better religion'. After talking to her, the witnesses gave her a Bible and urged her to read it. She did so, and this led her to a saving faith in the Lord Jesus Christ. [20] Another real source of encouragement was the Orphanage. Two boys had been placed in farms, one boy was studying at the College for Engineers in Paimpol, while another boy had started his career at sea.[21]

DEVELOPMENTS IN PAIMPOL

The Pioneer Mission was concerned for the safety of Caradoc Jones and his fellow labourers in Paimpol. The London office sent a telegram to Brittany calling all British subjects to return to Britain.[22] The telegram did not arrive, but even if Caradoc Jones had received the message he would not have left. He was determined to stay in Paimpol. He did, however, arrange for three of the members, Mrs Chapallez, her son, Henry and Edna Jones, his niece, to leave.[23]

Henry had already booked his passage, but Caradoc Jones spent some time in persuading the skipper to take the two ladies. At the last moment they hurried aboard the two-masted yacht, just before 6 o'clock on the evening of 9 June 1940, a day before Italy joined Germany in the war and a fortnight before Paris fell. There were about fifty persons on board, most of them young men that had started studying to join the French Navy. It took the yacht sixteen hours to cross to England, but in spite of the length of time, the journey was comparatively easy.[24] Mrs Chapallez, sad at leaving the fellowship at Paimpol, found peace of mind in a verse of Scripture that had come to her mind before leaving: 'A thousand shall fall at thy side, and ten thousand at thy right hand, but it shall not come nigh thee' (Psalm 91:7).[25] All of them were glad to arrive, and Henry Chapallez was able to visit the Pioneer Mission centre on 24 June to give the most recent news concerning Paimpol. Edna Jones continued on her journey back to Ponciau, Wrexham, and in a short while married James Evans, a Scotch Baptist.[26] She continued in the tradition of that denomination, while Caradoc Jones kept in touch with it through his family. He had to continue in Paimpol without the company of some of his best friends.

113

ARRIVAL OF THE GERMANS

Caradoc Jones, and some others in Paimpol, for reasons not mentioned, did not think that the Germans would reach that part of Brittany.[27] After the fall of France, that was inevitable. The Germans moved westward aiming for St Malo, Brest and St Nazaire. Capturing these centres would give them control of the whole of Brittany. Already on 15 June 1940, the British had decided on the evacuation of Allied troops in the three ports mentioned and others as well.[28] Altogether 156,000 persons were evacuated from French harbours. Brittany was not well defended and it was imperative that no time was lost. A mere eighty soldiers with small arms defended St Malo, and although there were two defense-lines outside Brest, they would not be able to withstand the German attack.

On 18 June, St Malo and Brest were evacuated. From St Malo 21,474 were evacuated and 22,584 from Brest. It is a marvel that the company left Brest because, in a short time, the channel was crowded with warships and cargo ships.[29] Others made their own arrangements. For example, one hundred and thirty fishermen from Ille de Sens left before the Germans arrived. They crossed to Portsmouth and later joined the Free French Naval Force.[30]

The war continued because Winston Churchill would not agree to any peace terms. As the result of the German occupation of France, there was the possibility of an attack on Britain. [31] Before that could take place, Germany had to gain ascendancy in the air, but that was made impossible after her defeat in the Battle of Britain. During this period Britain was heavily bombed, especially London, Plymouth, Coventry and Swansea.[32] But the British Air Force overcame the attack of the Luftwaffe (German Air Force). The victory brought forth one of Winston Churchill's quotable sayings: 'Never in the field of human conflict was so much owed by so many to so few'.[33] It was different in France. The Germans were in control of that country and they had reached Brittany with grave consequences for the church at Paimpol.

114

BESANÇON INTERNMENT CAMP

The Germans reached Paimpol. German cars were patrolling the streets and German soldiers were making inquiries concerning the activities of some of the inhabitants, including Caradoc Jones. They wanted to know if he was using his radio, and it was also reported that 'an Alsacian woman secretary had been seen with a German officer making notes of the times of the services'.[34]

It was not long before the German officers visited Caradoc Jones personally. The State Police (SS) arrived, or the Gestapo as they were called. They emerged in 1933 under the guidance of Hermann Goring and Heinrich Himmler. They operated without any civil restraints and had the power to imprison and to put to death. Jews and Gypsies suffered terribly at the hands of the Gestapo, especially during the war. On 1 December 1940 they called on Caradoc Jones. It was a Sunday, and the pastor had prepared a message on Jeremiah 45:5, 'Seekest thou great things for thyself? Seek them not-but thy life I will give unto thee for a prey in all places whither thou goest'. [35] As Caradoc Jones was coming downstairs, ready to go to the church, Mme. Matthews informed him that a man was at the door asking for the pastor. The man was a member of the Gestapo and uttered just one word, 'Come'. The pastor was denied the opportunity to preach that morning and even his request to collect some clothes was refused.[36]

Caradoc Jones was taken to a house on the west- side of the harbour, 'locked in a room that was in darkness owing to a closed iron shutter outside the window. Its furniture consisted mainly of an iron bedstead and a piece of blanket'.[37] A boy from the orphanage recognized Caradoc Jones in the car and told the members of the church. They found out where the pastor was being kept and brought him some food. After four days in the house, the captive was taken to St Brieuc. Once again it was found out where he was kept and members of the church told friends in St Brieuc of what had happened. They visited him and brought him some gifts.[38]

115

After five days in St Brieuc, Caradoc Jones was taken to an internment camp in Besançon on the river Doubs, named Frontstalag 142. It was an internment camp, not a concentration camp like Auschwitz, Buchanwald or Belsen. The concentration camps were for enemy soldiers but the internment camps were for civilians in an occupied country, like France. In a few weeks Besançon was overcrowded with 2,400 persons with 500 elderly housed in St Jacques Hospital. Groups arrived from different places, including Paris and Brittany.[39] One of the internees from Paris said that on arrival 'We were led to a massive sombre building; the barracks gate opened and we crossed a filthy, muddy court-yard and were told to go into the building'.[40]

Caradoc Jones and others from Brittany arrived in heavy rain and were left to themselves to look for a bed. The pastor found one with difficulty after being helped by the Rev. H. H. Pullen of the Spezia Mission. It wasn't really a bed that Caradoc Jones found. It was a mattress that he placed on the floor between two beds. H. H. Pullen had been working with the Spezia Mission in Italy. He had left Italy and journeyed to Paris but arrived when the Germans captured the city. At the camp he became the Protestant chaplain and met with a small group of believers around a stove in a large room.[41] This was an interesting meeting because Pullen, like Caradoc Jones, was a former Spurgeon's College student.

The diet was usually black bread, but there was soup as well, that was not very appetizing as one of the internees explained, writing from the camp:[42]

> The soup when seen in the filthy tremendous tub in the kitchen for the first time, and soldiers throwing pails of water into it and stirring it round with a huge piece of wood is far from appetizing but we all appreciate it as it was hot and we are hungry.

The sanitary arrangements were utterly inadequate and the internees took time to cope with the lack of privacy.

Soon, the presence of the pastor was felt and even the most godless would be careful of their language when he was around. Most of those in the camp were without hope and without God in the world. Caradoc Jones joined H. H. Pullen in arranging services: 'By the second Sunday he had begun to organize regular services and meetings. He sought out singers, formed and trained a choir, and encouraged the members to write out hymns from memory'.[43] Caradoc Jones prepared for Christmas by practising carols, some of which he had written himself and arranged to popular tunes. They met in a room without windows in very cold weather and with snow outside. For tea on Christmas Day, the pastor had kept some fruit given to him in St Brieuc and, even after sharing, it was still a feast for many of the internees.[44] For a while they could forget the celery soup provided by drunken cooks. Parcels from the Red Cross made another Christmas day.

Other internees refer to the cold weather. The ladies were expected to wash in what appeared to be 'a large trough for cattle, except for a tap here and there, often frozen or adorned with icicles'.[45]

Not only was the general condition of the camp bad, Caradoc Jones also found out that his mattress was damp. This caused health problems:[46]

At first, unrealized by Mr Jones was the fact that his mattress was damp while all he had for a covering were two small, dirty blankets. For three weeks he had slept in his entire suit of clothes, and had woken each morning with pains all over his body and coughing badly. It brought on a severe attack of bronchitis which kept him in the infirmary for six weeks.

Another internee provides an answer to the damp mattress. On arrival they had been taken to[47]

Huge empty rooms, wet everywhere, we quickly ventured to the second floor. There it was just the same. Later we learnt that twenty thousand prisoners of war had recently left the barracks and had been ordered to throw pails of water down to clean the stone floors. The straw mattresses were literally floating. My friend found an old garden broom and swept the water away.

Caradoc Jones must have had a mattress that had not dried out thoroughly. After his recovery, Caradoc Jones rejoined H. H. Pullen, but he was taken ill and the Welshman took responsibility for all the work.[48]

One privilege that Caradoc Jones enjoyed was to visit the hospital two miles from the camp. Under escort he would visit the mothers and children twice a week. On no account was he to take messages out of the hospitals. On one occasion he was persuaded to do so and hid it on his body. When he came out, the escort had left. Another escort was found for him and they walked the two miles back to the camp, cold and very hungry because he had only been allowed a small ration of black bread that day. On arrival he was searched but the message was not found.[49] He was taking a tremendous risk in doing what he did and he knew very well what the consequences might have been. He could have suffered by the withdrawal of rations, moved to an even worse camp and possibly his life would have been in danger.

Caradoc Jones and the other internees were glad to leave Besançon. At 2 o'clock, one morning in May 1941, they were told to prepare to leave and did so three hours later. They were on their way to Vittel in the Vosges.[50]

1. For the War, Winston S. Churchill, *The Second World War* (vols. 1 and 2, London, 1949).
2. Winston Spencer Churchill was Prime Minister from 1940 to 1945. Numerous books have been written on his life and work. Three recent works: John Strawson, *Churchill and Hitler in Victory and Defeat* (First published in Great Britain, Constable, London, 1997); Geoffrey Best, *Churchill: A Study in Greatness* (Penguin Books, 2001); Paul Adams, *The Unexpected Hero* (Oxford University Press, 2005).
3. James F. McMillan, *Twentieth-Century France* (Edward Arnold, 1992 ed.), 127.
4. Philip Warner, *The Battle of France 1940* (Cassell & Co. 2001 ed.), ch. 10; Julian Jackson, *The Fall of France* (Oxford U.P, 2003), 95.
5. Churchill gives the number of vessels as 861 and lists different kinds of British ships; how many were sunk, and how many damaged, *The Second World War*, Volume Two, 97; ibid., gives 'Accumulated Total' of Allied troops landed in England as 338, 226, 108. John Strawson believed that 'The "miracle" of Dunkirk was an astonishing affair', *Churchill and Hitler*, 261.
6. Churchill, *The Second World War*, 138-9. Charles de Gaulle (1890-1970) was the self-appointed leader of the Free French settled in England. Later became Prime Minister of France and then President of the Fifth Republic. For his work during the early years of the War: 'France and de Gaulle', Geoffrey Best, *Churchill: A Study in Greatness*. Marshal Pétain (1856-1951) was a hero during 1914-8 War, but he negotiated peace with Germany in 1940 and became a 'German puppet'. He was later found guilty of treason, sentenced to death, but commuted to life imprisonment: John Strawson, *Churchill and Hitler*, xxvi.
7. G1–World War II Commemoration: viewed 30/6/04. The period from May 1940 until June 1941 is regarded as Churchill's finest hour: 'The title often and justly conferred upon him as the Saviour of the nation rests above all on how he managed the war and kept the country going and its people united through the period from May 1940 until June 1941', Geoffrey Best, *A Study in Greatness*, 169.
8. Web site Guardian Unlimited, 1940 Paris falls to the Germans: viewed 20/12/04.
9. Jackson, *The Fall of France*, 176.
10. Ibid.
11. Ibid., 174.
12. Vichy France: McMillan, *Twentieth-Century France*, III, 13.
13. 1 Rue Amelot:Rescue as Resistance, France, 1940-1944: viewed14/10/05.
14. McMillan, *Twentieth-Century France*, 135.
15. 'Holding the Fort at Paimpol', *The Pioneer Review*, April-June, 1940; ibid., 'Paimpol', January-March, 1940.
16. Ibid.
17. Ibid., 'Paimpol', January-March, 1940.

18. Ibid., 'Holding the Fort at Paimpol', April-June, 1940.
19. Ibid.
20. Ibid.
21. Ibid.
22. Ibid., 'Brittany', July-Septe0mber, 1940.
23. *Knight in Royal Service*, 35; information from Mrs Edna Evans, né Jones, Ponciau.
24. Ibid. 'Latest Paimpol News', July-September, 1940
25. Ibid.
26. Information Mrs Edna Evans, né Jones, Ponciau.
27. *Knight in Royal Service*, 35.
28. Churchill, *The Second World War*, 168.
29. Philip Warner, *The Battle of France*, 221.
30. World at War.net/article.Brittany: viewed 20/9/04.
31. Philip Warner, *The Battle of France*, III, 22. The occupation created financial difficulties for Caradoc Jones: 'Mr Phillips also reported that owing to the enemy occupation of Brittany, it was now impossible to send money to the Rev. Caradoc Jones', Angus Library, Sub-Committee, 20 June 1943.
32. Details for Wales: John O'Sullivan, *When Wales Went to War, 1939-45* (Sutton Publishing, 2004); 387 killed in Swansea, 355 in Cardiff, 3.
33. 'Primer's Review of the War', *The Guardian*, 21 August 1940
34. *Knight in Royal Service*, 36.
35. Ibid.
36. Ibid., 37.
37. Ibid.
38. Ibid.
39. Website: NZETC-Prisoners of War-III:Civilians in Europe: 16/7/04.
40. Imperial War Museum, London: 'Miss Bayliss Memoir', 5, deposited 1996.
41. *Knight in Royal Service*, 38.
42. 'Miss Bayliss Memoir', 10.
43. *Knight in Royal Service*, 38.
44. Ibid. 39. Another aspect of camp life was the noise: 'Owing to the number in the room, silence was rare, so we imposed upon ourselves a silent hour, 1.30 to 2.30 in the afternoon', Miss Bayliss Memoir, 16.
45. 'Miss Bayliss Memoir', 9.
46. *Knight in Royal Service*, 39.
47. 'Miss Bayliss Memoir', 5.
48. *Knight in Royal Service*, 39-40.
49. Ibid., 40-1.
50. 'Miss Bayliss Memoir', 22. 'In May 1941, the Germans moved the internees to Vittel under pressure from Winston Churchill who told the German authorities through the Red Cross that if living conditions were not improved quickly, the government would consider transferring German civilians imprisoned in Britain to the north of Canada', 87PDF.

7

VITTEL AND PAIMPOL
1940-46

Vittel, like Besançon, was an internment camp, but there was a marked difference between the buildings in the two places. There was an unusual arrangement in Vittel, because the Germans had possessed a number of hotels and had transformed them into a camp, named Frontstalag 194, covering an area of 450,000 metres.[1] All but one of the hotels were on the same location and the Germans guarded the passage between this hotel and the other hotels. Within was a large park containing a garden and open spaces. The place was encircled by barbed wire and German patrols were on constant guard. The internees included British and American citizens and Jews from Poland, Holland and Belgium, mainly, but there were others from a number of other countries.[2]

The internees from Britain were found in four hotels, the majority of them in the Grand Hotel:[3]

British:
Grand Hotel	822
Vittel-Palace	41
Continental	333
Sources	293

The Americans arrived 29 September 1942 and were placed in Central Hotel, but two of them were sent to the Grand Hotel. This Hotel was the centre of British activity and it was here that Caradoc Jones was interned, prisoner number 117. It was a huge five-story

121

building with two long wings, able to accommodate a thousand internees.[4] Although the Germans had taken most of the furniture, the place was in excellent condition and spacious. It had three kitchens, the largest for the bulk of the internees, one for children and those with special needs and another for making tea.[5] Numerous bathrooms were found throughout the spacious hotel. Adjacent to the Grand Hotel was the Palace Hotel that was turned into a hospital. Numbers for the whole camp fluctuated. In 1942 it was 1,779; in 1943, 2,267 and for one period it was over 3,000. When liberated the number was 2,087.[6]

The camp was strictly organized:[7]

Grand Hotel	centre of British activity
Continental	old men, British and American women, including nuns
Sources	family camp
Central	mostly American, 2 British
New Hotel	family camp
Hotel Pasteur	maternity home
Villa Thermes	for delicate women
Palace Hotel	for doctors and patients
Hopital Mareval	for mental cases
Providence Hotel	Jews

Most of the internees were from Britain, including a few from Wales. One of them, Miss Gladys Jeffreys, Newport, managed to escape from the camp in August 1941.[8] Another Welsh person was mentioned. A lady internee had a new room-mate: 'My new room-mate was Welsh, black-eyed, with thick black hair, parted in the front and drawn like curtain over her forehead, short, stubby and inclined to be bandy-legged'.[9] She had spent thirty years in the service of a French family. Early in the war, the husband of the family and one of the sons were killed and another son taken prisoner.

These events and her own capture affected the Welsh girl because she acted very strangely in camp. She had an obsession with keeping the windows open even in the cold weather.[10] She was argumentative and stubborn and in a short time was a nuisance in the camp. No wonder that she was called the 'crow'.[11]

HUMANE CONSIDERATIONS AND REAL SUFFERING

As it was an internment camp, the internees did not experience the barbarity of the concentration camps. There were no mass killings and no gas chambers. Efforts were made to treat the internees humanely. Compared with Besançon it was a luxury to have water from a tap and to have sheets on the bed.[12] A most important aspect of the arrangements was to keep the families together.[13] Consequently, the children could attend the school set up in the camp.

Opportunities were given for all kinds of activities and as one internee commented: 'It was surprising as years passed, the talent discovered among the internees'.[14] A drama group was formed and succeeded in producing one of Bernard Shaw's plays. A number of instrumentalists, especially violinists and pianists, performed in concerts. A number of instruments were received from the YMCA in Paris. Considering the situation, a good library was set up in the Grand Hotel.[15] A number of artists, amateur and professional, were among the internees. Many of them had their own studios. One artist worked in an ugly room, but his delight was painting primroses and he also planted primroses in Red Cross tins.[16] Many women spent much of their free time in sewing and produced astonishing work.[17] There was opportunity for physical exercises like walking in the park and tennis became very popular with the internees. Less strenuous was a visit to the cinema or meeting to play Bridge.[18] The internees had no problem at all in arranging an exhibition of the work done in the camp. One item that Caradoc Jones valued was a tablecloth, made of old flour sacks and presented to him at the camp. He was able to keep it safe and bring it out when the camp was liberated.[19]

But in spite of all the humane considerations, Vittel was an internment camp. The place was overcrowded and, as in Besançon, one of the great difficulties was the lack of privacy. Although sanitary conditions were better than in the previous place, they were not what they should be even in an internment camp. During the early days many of the internees had been allowed to bring their dogs with them, but there was no separate place to keep them, and three Scotch sisters kept their dog in the bathroom. In many rooms, mice were uninvited guests.[20] The amount of food was insufficient and the quality poor. This was true of the potatoes, the porridge and the soup. The meat provided on Sundays would slip away under the knife and it was only with effort that the cabbage could be eaten.[21]

Occasionally there would be further cuts. At one time the soup allowed for the mid-day meal was four spoonfuls. The margarine allowance at the beginning of 1942 was 90 grs per person per week. By the end of the year it was cut o 12 grs 50. This can be compared with ration time in Britain. Each person was allowed 2 oz of butter per week. In Britain it was possible to have 4 oz of bacon and egg and a shilling's worth of meat (10p), while in Vittel at the end of 1942 they only had 3 oz of either meat or sausage.[22]

THE JEWS

Jews, especially, had a reason for detesting the place. Many of them were brought there for a period and then moved on to concentration camps. To them, Vittel was a transit camp. Knowing the attitude of the Germans, they often panicked if a command came for them to leave, because that meant probable death. Many were carried to hospital: 'Some had poisoned themselves, some cut arteries, one woman threw herself from the fifth floor window, she had several young sons and her husband was in England, these events caused a general depression in the camp'.[23]

124

Amongst those that spent some time in Vittel were many Jewish authors and leaders. They included Yitzhak Katzenelson, poet and dramatist.[24] His wife and two of the children died in the Warsaw Ghetto. Katzenelson himself, and one son, were taken from Warsaw to Vittel, where they occupied room 107 and then taken to Auschwitz, where both of them died. The experiences at Vittel are poignantly portrayed in his work, *Vittel Diary.*[25]

Another Jew was Professor Schorr who, with his wife and daughter, were transferred from Warsaw to Vittel. They thought that they were being exchanged for German prisoners of war, but they were kept in Vittel for one year and then told that they would be moved to Drancy transit camp. They were alarmed because they knew that the ultimate destination would be Auschwitz. The wife committed suicide and the daughter was severely injured when she attempted suicide by jumping from a window. They acted in this way in order to protect the children of the daughter. They knew that if the children were orphans they would not be taken to Drancy or Auschwitz.[26]

Winifred Pierce recalls what one period of suffering meant to Caradoc Jones and others in the camp:[27]

The memory of one period in Vittel remains a nightmare of horror. There were some 300 Jews and Jewesses in the camp. And when they were segregated from the rest of the internees they knew that this was the first step towards their doom. Some of them threw themselves to death from fifth-floor windows. When the men were marched off by night to a nearby train panic broke out among the women, and Nurse Thompson was sent for. She telephoned to the doctor to bring sleeping tablets. He came and put them all to sleep.

It was a harrowing experience.

The Nurse Thompson mentioned in the account had a room next door to Caradoc Jones on the ground floor. It overlooked the main road and the beauty outside contrasted with the ugliness inside, because 'Beyond is a green park, with trees and shrubs which are at present all red and gold'.[28] Nurse Thompson was working with the Red Cross in Paris when the Germans captured the city. In the camp she was appointed supervisor of the Infirmary.[29] She nursed Caradoc Jones during a time of illness. Through his witness she was converted and was the mainstay of his support at the camp. After liberation day, that support continued until Caradoc Jones' death.

CAMP MEETINGS
In spite of uncertainties and difficulties, Caradoc Jones resolved to hold regular services. There was religious provision for the camp, for Roman Catholics, Church of England and Jews. In spite of the attitude to the Jews, a synagogue was set up in Providence Hotel in 1943. [30] Caradoc Jones was one of six people that held services in the camp. By the second Sunday after his arrival, he was ready to lead the worship. The Commandant co-operated willingly and provided a suitable room, 'lined with mirrors, which the missionary accepted with a whimsical smile'.[31] Winifred Pearce provides further information:[32]

> Next came the question of furnishing, and the officer met every one of the not inconsiderate requests for two hundred chairs, a platform for the choir, an organ and a pulpit. For the last he found a cashier's desk which served the purpose admirably. As an organist and counsellor of women converts he had the able assistance of Miss Le Page of Guernsey, again Mr. Jones found himself involved in a great missionary enterprise, with services and meetings every day of the week.

The internees lived mainly on black bread but that was no reason for not remembering Harvest time. Caradoc Jones obtained vegetables and fruit from the canteen and arranged a Harvest Thanksgiving Service.[33]

The aim of all missionary work was twofold: to reach as many as possible with the gospel and to provide fellowship for believers. Those who professed faith in Christ were received into membership, because Caradoc Jones was convinced that he should work on personal and church levels. The Treasurer of the Pioneer Mission reported to the Council 'That he [Caradoc Jones] told of enthusiastic fellowship in service, with conversions and additions to the Church'.[34] The missionary knew that God was at work and that, therefore, there was a great need for prayer: 'I received six members into fellowship on confession of faith a month ago and two on Sunday last. Plead for prayers and more prayers on our behalf'.[35]

A lady that understood the nature of the gospel for the first time during her stay in the camp was the organist, Le Page. Writing to the *Review,* she gave an account of some aspects of the work:[36]

> Mr Jones often told us about Wales and about the Welsh revivals, and we were always praying for revival in the camp. Perhaps they will get it yet. There is a group of young girl converts, ten or fifteen, and they hold daily prayer meetings among themselves. I was not of their number, because I am advanced in age (50), but a number of older persons, like me, had come over into the evangelical group out of various denominations. Needless to say, there is plenty of opposition, and Mr Jones is working hard against tremendous odds. He has a little help now. Since the arrival of Colonel Estil of the Salvation Army, and Mr Gamble from Poland, and of course Mr Stamp.

Apart from personal work, Miss le Page was responsible for a daily Bible study. Caradoc Jones was active himself and also knew how to delegate responsibility.

Another internee bears witness to the good influence of Caradoc Jones. She had been arrested in Paris, and with others, were 'herded like cattle' into a small room in Vittel camp. She shared the 'evil-smelling food' and had to keep clean without soap. The lady was unsettled and longed for something to help her in such a camp and decided to go to hear the Nonconformist pastor:[37]

> How cold was the room in which the meetings were held! Every one was stiff with cold, yet we came to feel we could not miss a service. Pastor Jones never missed a service, yet how he could stand the cold was amazing seeing that he was seventy years of age! I can see his grave, sweet face still explaining Christ's great sacrifice. His message filled us with hope; hope so necessary to us in our sadness, and for lack of which some poor women actually lost their reason.

It was through these services that the lady was able to 'openly and fully accept Christ'. Another one had been won for Christ and for the camp church.

Some opposed the work, others were sarcastic in referring to the 'Evangelist'. One lady internee listed the religious provision for the camp, including: 'The Evangelist minister and his flock of angels, such sweet girls, who must neither play tennis nor dance nor go to plays or the pictures, and appeared quite contented to sing hymns'.[38]

Miss Le Page was one of the 'sweet girls'. She was one of a group of six ladies converted in the camp. The six of them were repatriated and returned to Britain. They reached Cardiff, and attended a meeting at Gabalfa Baptist Church, where Caradoc Jones had ministered before leaving for Brittany.[39] In a meeting in Gabalfa, Miss Le Page and Miss Millward gave their personal testimony and F. J. Legge, the pastor, baptized four of the group. It must have been a great joy for the church at Gabalfa to witness the fruit of Caradog Jones' ministry in Vittel. There were bonuses as well. Another lady in the group expressed her desire to be baptized; three from the church were converted, 200 friends stayed for tea and a collection realized £90-10-6.[40]

The Red Cross would make up lists of what was needed in the camp, and one list included a request from Caradoc Jones:[41]

Wanted for the Evangelical Church – Rev. Caradoc Jones
10 Large Print English Bibles
60 New Testaments (English)
An assortment of books to circulate among Christian girls
'Slives' (probably author's name) of Bible Lands
                                                          Bible studies
                                                          Missionary work ₵

A note was included in the margin suggesting 'Slides' for 'Slives'. Someone had made a mistake with 'Slides'. During a visit to the Camp, YMCA representatives drew up a list of requests that they had received, including:[42]

for Mr Jones
          20 Pilgrim's Progress (Bunyan) in French or English
          5 Bibles English.
          10 translations of L. Segond – in French

The requests reveal how anxious the pastor was to teach the believers and to have them read and understand the Scriptures.

Apart from the strange location and the ill health of many of the internees, Caradoc Jones had to struggle with his own physical weakness. He had been very ill for five weeks, almost immediately before being arrested by the Gestapo. During his stay in Besançon, he spent six weeks in hospital. He had brief periods of ill health in Vittel, the most serious early in 1943. He wrote to his relatives in Ponciau saying that he was not well. Writing again a little later to James and Edna Evans, né Jones, his niece, 2 March 1943, he referred to his illness:[43]

Kriefsgefangenenlager
Camp des prisonniers   March 2nd/43

You will be expecting a word from me, although I wrote you last
month & have not received one from you. I wrote to Bryn Offa
a week or two ago. Hope you receive the same. Well, I was
saying then that I was unwell, & so I was, very; I had to keep to
bed for a month with only getting up to preach twice in the
month. However, am glad to say that through the mercy of God
I am much better & can go out daily and am taking the Services
gradually.
                                   Yrs Caradoc

His ruling passion was to preach the gospel.

Most of his co-workers were with Caradoc Jones for most of the
time in Vittel. He was fortunate that they were not moved to another
place. Caradoc Jones was also glad to see a fellow Welshman
arriving, in spite of the fact that he was a prisoner. He was Kenneth
Mervyn Thomas from Swansea, who was Professor of English in the
English Institute, Prague, when the War broke out. He spent some
time in Bratislava where 'they slept like rats on a stone floor' and fed
with 'black potatoes and appalling bread'.[44] He arrived in Vittel in
February 1944, to teach English to the internees and remained there
until liberated eight months later.[45]

Caradoc Jones was happy when any of the internees, including his
co-workers, were repatriated. He himself had an opportunity to
leave on several occasions. Part of one of his letters was read in a
Council meeting, 'in which he reported that some 6 or 8 of his
Church members would be leaving shortly for the homeland. He
stated that he could be with them, but was staying in order to keep
in touch with his work.'[46]

LIBERATION

When Caradoc Jones was writing his letter to the Council, the Allied forces were preparing to land in Normandy, bent on conquering France and recapturing Paris. The time was ripe to do so. The invasion of Britain had not materialized and America had joined Britain in the war. Hitler had turned his attention to Russia. The Allies adopted a well-known military method, that of misleading the enemy. On 5 June 1944, General Hans Cramer, a German officer, arrived in Berlin. He had been captured in Tunisia during May 1943 and taken to a Prisoner of War Camp in Wales. One of his co-prisoners was General Vaerst, who was taken to Island Farm Camp in Bridgend, south Wales. It is not certain if Cramer was taken there. Because of ill health he was repatriated. Cramer was misled regarding the journey home and he thought that they were in south-east England, while, actually, they were in London. On his arrival in Germany he reported that the Allies were preparing to cross to Calais.[47]

On 6 June 1944, British, American, Canadian and Polish troops began 'Operation Overlord' and landed in Normandy. They gained victory but had to fight fiercely and suffered huge losses.[48] Allied troops advanced westward, captured Cherbourg and moved to liberate Brittany. In a few months' time opposition was overcome, with only pockets of resistance in Lorient and St Nazaire. St Brieuc was liberated on 5 August, Guingamp on the 16th, and Paimpol on the 17th of the month.[49] Large numbers of German troops had retreated to the Paimpol area and were not easily overcome. It needed the combined effort of the French Resistants, Allied Air Force and American troops to do so. The liberation was led by Henry de Mauduit, lord of the Manor Bourblanc. He and his friend, Gaston Antébi, took part in the liberation of Paris a few days later.[50]

Other allied troops marched towards Paris. The US 4th Infantry approached from the east and the 2nd Armoured Division from the west. Dietrich von Choltitz, in command in Paris, contrary to

Hitler's directive surrendered to the Allied troops. It is one of the 'ifs' of history to think of what might have happened if Choltitz had obeyed. There would have been mass destruction, bridges, museums, the Louvre, the Eiffel Tower, houses and parks would have been destroyed. Torpedoes, kept in a tunnel under the city, if released would destroy huge parts of the city. Choltitz disobeyed because of the possible barbarity, because many Germans would be killed and because Paris was the 'city of light'.[51]

It had been arranged for the 2nd Armoured Division, under General Leclerc, to enter the city first. It was part of the American 3rd Army.[52] The Friends' Ambulance Unit was attached to the Armoured Division. One of the men working with the Division was the pacifist, A. Tegla Davies, son of Tegla Davies, well known in Wales as a minister and an author.[53] A. Tegla Davies and his co-workers joined the march towards Paris, relieved, but exhausted after long hours of attending to the wounded. A person who was present described the scene:[54]

> We were kissed, hugged, praised and prayed over; we got glasses of wine, handful of apples, and a flag to tie to the bonnet of the car. In return we gave away the cigarettes, biscuits and sweets we had been saving for this very occasion, and their delight at these little things was something one doesn't easily forget. And always as we moved away we heard that, most heart-warming of all send offs – 'Bon courage, mes enfants!' As we came round a bend down in the valley below we saw Paris glowing in the last rays of the setting sun and the Eiffel Tower pointing its lean finger upwards into the mist.

In Paris itself there was triumphant rejoicing and even the members of the Friends' Ambulance Unit took off their hats.

More work was to be done by the Unit as they found the hospitals overcrowded. They also had to find room for the wounded they had picked up on the way.

After about ten days in Paris they were on the move again and left on the 8 September, marching in the direction of Strasbourg, aiming for Germany. The Allies gained victories at Metz and Nancy and continued in the direction of Contrexeville and Vittel. [55] The Friends' Unit was still travelling with the troops. Vittel was taken and two internee camps were discovered, one at Vittel itself and the other at Clermont. Between the two camps there were altogether 4,300 internees. Vittel was taken on the 12 September: 'So we come to the 12 September on which date the Leclerc Division liberated us after a bombardment of 1000 shells of 105 cal. which caused comparatively slight damage to Vittel and none at all in the Camp itself which was carefully spared'.[56] At 6 o'clock in the evening General Leclerc arrived to greet the Anglo-American internees.[57]

One of the Friends described the scene in Vittel:[58]

T xt T [Casualty Clearing Station] had one or two moves through Lorraine, through the spa town of Contrexeville, and thence to Vittel, where there was a flood of casualties – French, Maquis, Germans and civilians. In a large hotel, Section Rouge [another division within the Unit] operated through the night, until seven o'clock in the morning, had three hours' sleep, and then at ten began again. The corridors were blocked with wounded, and operations went on into the small hours of the following morning.

Vittel, including the internment camp, had been liberated. Working untiringly, little did A. Tegla Davies know that there were a few Welshmen among the internees, including Caradoc Jones and Kenneth Mervyn Thomas from Swansea. Two civil Affairs detachments, assisted by the American Red Cross, supervised the care of the internees, who were longing to leave Vittel. The place had been taken on 12 September 1944, but a few weeks passed before all the internees were released. The aim was to complete the evacuation by 23 October. Because of the shortage of food in Paris, all internees destined for the capital were provided with at least one British or American Red Cross parcel.[59] Caradoc Jones had to wait to the end and felt lonely as most from the church had already left the camp: 'I fear that my turn for Brittany will be the last'. When released he was determined to return to Paimpol before visiting Wales, but assured his relatives that he longed for 'Gwalia annwyl' (dear Wales).[60]

1944-6

The day of his release did arrive. Nurse Thompson, who, as we noted above, had been converted in camp, accompanied him to Paris and then to Paimpol. Arthur Matthews had already arrived from the south of France. Caradoc Jones was able to write to Rhos from Paimpol:[61]

> Here at last! Left Vittel on October 23rd. Hundreds, if not thousands left for Bourbonvulle, near Vichy, because they had no definite homes to go to – Poles, Russians, French, Algerians, English and Jews. I had to stay in Paris for a fortnight because my luggage had gone astray. Our people did not expect me until the next day. It was a surprise for them, and they and myself were glad to meet after a separation of four years. I am sitting at a nice wood fire, the first I have seen for ever so long. Not a scratch on the Manse, chapel or Orphanage, although the battle raged around Paimpol. God be praised for his goodness.

He was the last person to leave. He himself said that his health was as good as could be expected, but he was really quite weak:[62]

> Due to his experience in captivity heart trouble had developed, and his strength was utterly spent. At the gates he sank to the ground, unable to go further. A coloured girl who had been among the last to leave, saw his plight, and with her timely help he reached the station.

Caradoc Jones spent Christmas 1944 in Paimpol. They had a good meeting in the church in the afternoon devoted mainly to the children. They even managed to find gifts for them. The singing, especially the carols, were thoroughly enjoyed, but 'Our old carols had to do again, as I was not there to find and teach new ones'.[63]

The Orphanage had kept going without a hitch, but there was a need for food, clothes and shoes and there was a great need generally in the area. It was difficult to believe that there was hardly any butter in Brittany and difficult to get tea, coffee, milk and rice. This lack was made up by a supply of potatoes and fruit. Coal had not been available for a long time and wood was scarce, but they managed by cutting old trees and withered branches. It could not be worse than Vittel.[64]

In three months' time Caradoc Jones left for London. He arrived 14 February 1945, and paid a visit to the Pioneer Mission Council the following day.[65] He summarized the work that had been done in the internment camp, mentioning also his periods of ill health. Caradoc Jones proceeded and drew attention to some financial matters. He was willing to waive the six months salary due to him, but would be glad to receive £12, commencing January 1945. He also presented the case of his co-workers and believed that Mme Matthews should have £50 for the war period and Mr Huck £150 for the same period. Both sums could be regarded as loans until the Mission was in a position to pay the two sums. In future Caradoc Jones suggested £8 per month for Mr Matthews and £7 per month for Mr Huck.[66] The pastor did not forget his co-workers in spite of the fact that they had been apart for four years.

The ill effects of the internment camps had not cleared. On a visit to Dr. Martyn Lloyd-Jones, Westminster Chapel, London, on Sunday, 18 February 1945, Caradoc Jones was advised to rest.[67] He tried to follow the advice and spent some time in the home of one of his brothers in 'Craigfryn', Johnson Street, Ponciau, Wrexham. Although he was resting, he did take two meetings in Rhos. In the first one, at

Penuel Baptist church, he concentrated on his period in Besancon[68] and in the other meeting, at Capel Mawr, he related the events at Vittel.[69] In spite of the fact that he had been away for such a long time, the people of Rhos and the local paper warmly welcomed Caradoc Jones on his return home.

In three weeks' time he was on the move again, preaching and speaking on behalf of the Pioneer Mission. Places visited included Gabalfa Baptist church, Cardiff, and the Metropolitan Tabernacle in London. The Cardiff meeting was overcrowded and three hundred friends stayed for tea.[70] Many of those present had cherished memories of his ministry in their midst, and, of course, he had a thrilling story to tell them. In the meeting at the Metropolitan he summarized the account of what happened in Besançon and Vittel. Many in the Metropolitan remembered him from college days and from visits on behalf of the Pioneer Mission.[71]

During June, July and August, Caradoc Jones was busy travelling much in England and Wales. Early September he was in north Wales but by then he knew that he would have to go into hospital.[72] He entered Chesterfield Nursing Home in Clifton, Bristol. The specialist told him: 'I tell you frankly Mr Jones, if you had not come here you would have been dead in a very short time, but now you are good for ten years more'.[73] The treatment was a success and the Council was able to report 11 January 1946 that 'He was now prepared to book engagements for February and March with the hope of returning to Paimpol in April'. In the next meeting the Council was informed 'that up to the present time 18 engagements had been booked for the Rev. Caradoc Jones for the months of February and March of which 8 had been fulfilled with a result of £20-18-0'.[74] It was not possible for him to return in April, but he did leave for Paimpol in May 1946, and Nurse Thompson accompanied him. [75] At the beginning of the year Caradoc Jones had just celebrated his seventy-first birthday and his life was to be extended, not by ten, but by twenty-three years.

1. National Archives, Kew, FO916/634. Until January 1942 was named Font Stalag 121, FO 916/347.
2. National Archives, FO16/634;*Knight in Royal Service*, 41.
3. National Archives, FO916/634.
4. Ibid., and FO916/2612; HO215/68.
5. 'Workers helping in the kitchen got special privileges and were allowed to go as a group with a guard to the local village and buy things they needed. They also used to barter with the French farmers with their cigarettes and chocolates', WW2 People's War, viewed 12/10/06.
6. www.holocaustchronicle.org, viewed 15/12/04. National Archives, FO916/634 gives 2531 for December 1943 and 2080 when the camp was liberated.
7. National Archives, FO916/634; FO916/347. There were so many nuns in the Continental that it was called 'Camp Convent': Sisters recall their time as German prisoners, viewed 12/10/06.
8. National Archives, FO916/347.
9. Imperial War Museum, 'Miss Bayliss Memoir', 7.
10. Ibid., 8.
11. Ibid., 10.
12. Ibid., 2.
13. National Archives, FO916/634.
14. Imperial War Museum, 'Miss Bayliss Memoir', 14.
15. Ibid., 14-6. Another internee reported that 'in the Casino were performed Corneille, Moliere, Shakespeare and grand opera as they were pre-war. This residence was, nevertheless, forced and supervised', 87PDF.
16. Ibid., 23: 'All the ugliness was forgotten in an atmosphere of art and at the sight of a collection of Mr X's beautiful pictures'.
17. Ibid., 35.
18. National Archives, FO916/347; FO916/634.
19. Now in the hands of Mrs Beryl Hall, Cardiff.
20. Imperial War Museum, 'Miss Bayliss Memoir', 22.
21. Ibid., 39.
22. National Archives, FO916/634; c.f. Britain: *Reader's Digest Yesterday's Britain* (1998), 39.
23. Imperial War Museum, 'Miss Bayliss Memoir', 31-2. 'Recently [January 1943] there were several mental cases in the camp; 10 more serious cases were transferred to the mental hospital of Mareville in the neighbourhood', National Archives, FO916/634.
24. www.holocaustchronicle.org: viewed 15/12/04.
25. Ibid.
26. Ibid.
27. *Knight in Royal Service*, 42.
28. 'News from Brittany', *The Pioneer Review*, Autumn 1943.
29. National Archives, FO916/634; *Knight in Royal Service*, 42.
30. Imperial War Museum, FO916/634.
31. *Knight in Royal Service*, 41.

32. Ibid.
33. Ibid.
34. Angus Library, Special Council Meeting, 12 June 1942.
35. Quotation from a letter sent by Caradoc Jones, February 1943, in Angus Library, Scrap Book.
36. *The Pioneer Review*, Autumn 1943. Mr Stamp was from the church at Paimpol.
37. Translation of an article that appeared in *The British Advent Message*: 'Y Tufewn i Garchar', *Rhos Herald*, 17 February 1945.
38. Imperial War Museum, 'Miss Bayliss Memoir', 28.
39. Angus Library, Council Meeting, 11 October 1944, 63; cutting from *The Baptist Times*, 5 October 1944, Scrap Book; *Knight in Royal Service*, 41-2.
40. Angus Library, Council Meeting, 11 October 1944, 63.
41. National Archives, FO916/634.
42. Ibid., FO916.347.
43. Copy of the message in the author's possession, received from Edna Evans, né Jones, Ponciau; Council report: 'The Treasurer read a letter from the Rev. Caradoc Jones, in which he stated that he has had rather a bad time with heart trouble and has been obliged to rest, under Drs. orders, and to work a little less energetically in the future, and at the time of writing he expressed gratification for restoration'. Council Meeting, 11 May 1943; 'Mr Jones does not show much outward sign of a bad illness he had just over a year ago, but he suffers very severely from rheumatism, and his heart is somewhat weak', 'News from Brittany', *The Pioneer Review*, Autumn 1943
44. Angus Library, cutting of an article from the *Western Mail*, 18 October 1944: Scrap Book.
45. Ibid.
46. Ibid., Council Meeting, 19 May 1944, 51.
47. Deception and Disinformation-Psychological Operations, viewed 7/4/05; World War 2net, viewed 31/12/04.
48. Details given by Richard Holmes: *In The Footsteps of Churchill* (BBC Books, London, 2005), 264 It was during this period, on 30 June, that an attempt was made on Hitler's life. He reacted 'in a fit of frenzy' that led to a purging of leaders and the 'final subservience of the army to National Socialism', John Strawson, *Churchill and Hitler*, 431.
49. Dosiers-France 3 Ouest, viewed 5/1/05. Referring to Guingamp and Paimpol: 'Rammed by the armoured tanks and the fighter bombers, the two fortified towns go successively the 16 and August 17. 2,000 Germans made prisoners and given to the Americans by the resistant fighters', www.ouest.france3.fr/dossiers/4007647-fr.php; viewed 5/01/2005
50. 'An Allied Team with the French resistance', *Studies in Intelligence*, vol. 42, No. 2, 1998; Web site: Curriculum (S) Genealogy; viewed 15/12/2004.
51. History Channel.com, viewed 5/2/05.
52. As the result of an agreement between Churchill and de Gaulle, Geoffrey Best, *Churchill, A Study in Greatness*, 248.

53. A. Tegla Davies, *The Story of the Friends' Ambulance Unit 1939-46* (Allen and Unwin, London, 1947). For the father, E. Tegla Davies (1880-1967): Huw Ethall, *Tegla* (Swansea, 1980).
54. *The Story of the Friends' Ambulance Unit*, 163.
55. Ibid., 166.
56. National Archives, FO916/2612.
57. Ibid.
58. *The Story of the Friends' Ambulance Unit*, 167; they were in 'a world of rain and mud and dungheaps', ibid.
59. National Archives, WO219/1366.
60. Extract of letter from Caradoc Jones included in the *Rhos Herald*, 27 January 1945.
61. Ibid.
62. *Knight in Royal Service*, 42.
63. Extract of letter, *Rhos Herald*, 27 February 1945.
64. Ibid.
65. Angus Library, Council Meeting, 16 February 1945, 73.
66. Ibid.
67. Ibid., 23 March 1945; *Knight in Royal Service*, 43.
68. 'Rhyfeddodau o Gaeth-Wersyll', *Rhos Herald*, 14 April 1945.
69. Ibid., 21 April 1945.
70. Angus Library, Council Meeting, 10 May 1945, 77: 'The meeting at Mr. Jones' late church – Gabalfa – had proved an outstanding success. The building was filled to capacity on May 2nd, and 300 people were present at the Tea which was provided between the afternoon and evening gathering. Mr. Phillips was present as representative of the Mission'.
71. Ibid., 18 June 1945, 80.
72. Ibid., 16 July 1945, 82; 17 September 1945, 84.
73. *Knight in Royal Service*, 43.
74. Angus Library, Council Meeting, 22 February 1946, 93.
75. Ibid., 21 June 1946, 96.

8

NOT TOO OLD AT SEVENTY-ONE

Caradoc Jones was back in Paimpol: 'Here I am again at dear old Paimpol, and find very few changes, save around the beautiful coast, which has been badly scarred by German machinery and somewhat reduced in beauty by the ugly blockhouse. Still, there is beauty all round in this charming part of Brittany, especially at this time of year'.[1]

EARLY DAYS OF THE RETURN

Old friends joined Caradoc Jones in the work. Nurse Thompson became his housekeeper, Arthur Matthews returned from the south of France and Miss Cave was there ready to take charge of the orphanage. The chapel, manse and orphanage were not damaged during the war. The life of colporteur Huck could have been in danger because someone painted a De Gaulle's Cross of Lorraine on his house (a symbol of the Free French Movement). Providentially the Germans ignored it.[2] Others had been put to death for displaying such a symbol.

The returning pastor lost no time before taking up the reins again. He led the services during the first Sunday back in Paimpol, but the congregation was very different from that of previous years because fifty to sixty Germans were present. It had been arranged for Arthur Matthews to visit three military companies and Huck to visit another two companies. Those from Matthews' companies attended meetings at Paimpol. Some of the Germans who had come to Paimpol had been killed or wounded while demining the area around the coast. Those that attended the church worshipped reverently and enjoyed the German hymns. Arthur Matthews prayed in French and an interpreter read a message in German, prepared by Matthews.[3]

It was an emotional experience for Caradoc Jones to lead such a service. He himself revealed his feelings in a report to the *Pioneer Review*:[4]

> I could not but feel a strange tenderness pass over my heart as I looked into the faces of those men and recalled that Sunday morning when a Gestapo of their own race came to take me to captivity from the very same building and refused me the permission to preach a farewell sermon to our people; and now, here was I, privileged to preach to them in *their* captivity in the same building and to do so without any bitterness or hatred, but rather with the love of Christ which constrains us.

On the second Sunday in Paimpol, Caradoc Jones baptized three people. One was a lady who had been Charles Terrell's maid. She had listened to the gospel for a number of years but had not made any public profession of faith. The other two that were baptized with her were Gene, the adopted daughter of Miss Cave, and a young man converted under the ministry of Huck at Ste Barbe.[5] It was a great encouragement for Caradoc Jones to baptize three people, especially the young man. So many of the young people had left during the war, and the church was made up, mainly, of older people, widows and spinsters.

There were signs of change during 1950 and 1951. A few conversions took place and a few married couples joined the church. In the middle of July 1951, Caradoc Jones informed the Council that he had recently baptized four people.[6] The radical change that he would like to see was the coming of revival to Brittany and France. He had to deal with many tasks in Paimpol itself but he never lost sight of the need of the worldwide church. He urged the Council to

141

distribute copies of *Rent Heavens*, by R. B. Jones, Porth, Rhondda, and by April 1949, 700 copies had been distributed in many areas.[7] An order for 150 was received from the Keswick Depot in Melbourne.[8] A little later he expressed the same desire for revival, but this time in the form of a hymn, a translation by Dr William Edwards, Cardiff, of a well-known Welsh hymn: 'Pa le mae'r hen ymweliadau'. The opening line asked a question: 'Where are now the balmy breezes?' And the next verse opened with a prayer: 'Oh, my God and gracious Master, Send once more the copious showers'.[9] In Rhos, Cardiff, in the internment camp and in Paimpol, Caradoc Jones never forgot the supernatural dimension of revival.

Even an optimist like Caradoc Jones needed these tokens of blessing. Not only was he working immediately after the end of the war and after a period of ill health, he was also conscious of the presence of the Roman Catholic Church. He grasped every opportunity to expose what he believed to be Roman Catholic error. Caradoc Jones translated a booklet by the Swiss author, Faurre, entitled, *By Whom was the Church of Rome founded?* The pastor also recommended Faurre's *New Testament with Annotations*, and was delighted when Madame Faurre presented the Mission with 500 copies of the work, 'with the hope that the Roman Catholic teaching, especially during Holy Year might be somewhat counteracted and some financial gain might accrue to the Mission'.[10] The 500 copies arrived in London before 23 June 1950, to be sold at 3s-6d each. A Youth for Christ Rally was held in Paimpol, and Caradoc Jones felt it was 'a real achievement in such a strong Roman Catholic area'.[11] Mrs Matthews' mother came to live in the cottage held by the Pioneer Mission. Before she settled, assurances were received from the priests that she would have a Protestant funeral, although the mother was a nominal Roman Catholic.[12]

In spite of his opposition to Roman Catholicism, Caradoc Jones was always ready to meet with priests and people from the Roman Church. He was able to help a few priests with learning the Welsh language.[13] On one occasion the Protestant pastor accepted the suggestion of a priest that some of them from the Roman church should visit the Protestant Temple. Three priests and fourteen students from a nearby college came, but no account was given of the meeting. The pastor did inform the Council in London that the meeting had taken place and its response was recorded in a minute of 7 April 1961:

> Mr Jones' account of the visit of the three priests and fourteen students from a nearby College was read. It was received with mixed feelings, bearing in mind the duplicity of the Romish Church.

Caradoc Jones realized that the visitors would gain first hand information regarding Protestantism and that they could use that as a weapon to attack Protestantism. He also knew that they were there as visitors, not to take part in the service, and that he could explain the evangelical faith to them.

CARADOC JONES AND PIERRE LE SAUX

A close relationship was established between Caradoc Jones and one of the Roman Catholic priests. He was Pierre le Saux, who was brought up in a strict Roman Catholic home and was the son of an arranged marriage.[14] That arranged marriage, however, developed into a loving relationship, and the parents created a caring if strict home, for their children. As it was forbidden to speak Breton to the children, Pierre only heard French spoken in the home, but he would go to his grandparents and they insisted on speaking Breton to their grandchild. He was enabled to be bilingual.

As a young lad, Pierre would listen to Caradoc Jones preaching outside the school. Pierre listened intently and never left until the service came to an end. Caradoc Jones noticed him on several occasions and inquired concerning his background. Pierre left to attend a private school and after completing his higher education, prepared for the Roman Catholic priesthood. He was ordained at twenty-two years of age, one year earlier than the usual age for ordination. When war broke out in 1939, Pierre had to serve in the French Navy.[15]

Caradoc Jones and Pierre became very friendly during the years immediately after the war. During this period, Pierre was ministering within the Roman Catholic Church, but there was a strong tension in his life, resulting from the disharmony between his personal faith in Christ and his role as priest. He wanted to serve the Church but he was unhappy concerning three things. Pierre deplored the way that most of the priests dealt with the people. The priests were lording it over those given to their care. They were not servants. According to Pierre, the priests should be allowed to marry, and the other matter was the neglect of the Bible. The priests thought of it as a book for the Church and not for the people. Pierre wanted to see it in the hands of as many as possible.[16]

Pierre felt that he was a prisoner chained by the tradition of the Church. He shared his concern with Caradoc Jones and they decided on a bold plan. The pastor was to arrange the escape of Pierre from Brittany, without the knowledge of the priests. The destination was Wales via London. The first part of the plan was for Pierre to stay with Caradoc Jones for a few days, until arrangements were completed. When they had been finalized, Pierre cycled to the coast to catch a boat. The owner of the bicycle had been told where it would be left so that he could pick it up later.[17]

Arriving in London, Pierre found his way to Cardiff and visited the pastor of Tabernacle Welsh Baptist church, where there was strong support for the Paimpol Mission. Because of Pierre's background, the pastor advised him to join the Anglican Church and Pierre went to see the Bishop of Llandaff. He explained that it would take some time to establish the Breton priest in a church. The Bishop was aware of Pierre's views and they would not promote a good relationship between the Roman Church and the Church in Wales.

The Bishop was conscious of Pierre's broken English, and, also of his need to be instructed in the Church in Wales's teaching. To meet that latter need it was suggested that Pierre should spend twelve months in St Michael's College, Cardiff. The delay meant that he had no way of supporting himself and in order to earn some money worked as a porter on Cardiff Station.[18]

During this period he became interested in the history and literature of Wales. He attended the National Eisteddfod at Caerphilly, and spent some time in the company of Havard Gregory of Cardiff, who at the time was teaching English in Brittany. He had already met Caradoc Jones in Paimpol in 1947, when members of the Eisteddfod's Gorsedd visited Brittany.[19]

Pierre ministered for a while in St Fagan's and then moved to Splott, where he met his wife, Sylvia. He received a message from Brittany saying that his mother was ill and that he should return immediately. He went back and found that the news had been exaggerated. It was obvious that the family wanted him to stay in Brittany. He came back to Cardiff and the Bishop of Llandaff arranged for Pierre to serve a church in the Diocese of Fulham. His next sphere of labour was Lyon in France. It was arranged for him to work with the Anglican Church there and co-operate with the Old Catholic Church.[20]

Before he could start on his ministry, Pierre met with a serious accident and had to spend some time in hospital in Nice and Lyon. Because of complications after treatment to one of his legs, he had to recuperate in the mountains, where he had an opportunity to teach. During this period Pierre and his wife became acquainted with Graham Greene the novelist. After finishing in Lyon, Pierre and his wife returned to Brittany. They were able to buy a house because their daughter had won a prize for each of the three years that she had been in college. This must have been a great pleasure for them because for the whole time since Cardiff days, they had lived frugally.[21]

It was difficult for Pierre and Caradoc Jones to keep in touch regularly, but they did correspond. In his letters Caradoc Jones would always include verses from Scripture with appropriate comments. When Pierre was experiencing a period of suffering, Caradoc Jones referred him to the example of Job and urged him also to 'Turn to the Epistle to the Romans, chapter 8, and meditate on verses 37-9'. He should have the confidence of Paul, and thousands of other victorious saints, because 'nothing can separate you from the Love of God manifested in Jesus Christ'.[22]

FELLOW LABOURERS
Caradoc Jones shared the joys and problems of the work with his companions. He was especially glad that some of the early missionaries were still active. A reference to two of them, and to Caradoc Jones himself, was made in one of the Council meetings:[23]

> Mr. Matthews is a good Christian man and does not look his age [he would be in his mid-fifties at the time]. He is quiet and self-effacing. Mrs Matthews is a Frenchwoman and is really the 'boss'.

> Rev. C. Jones wants to 'die in harness'. He is not keen to have Americans to lead the work – he feels that a Welshman should be found.

> Mr Huck is 73 and frail. Mr Jones was not favourably impressed with him when he first went to Paimpol, but Mr Huck was in the work and has continued.

Mrs Matthews was still active in the Orphanage and Nurse Thompson was still the faithful housekeeper. Mr Stamp must have had a private income because when he retired in his 70s, he was able to offer £170 per annum and living accommodation to a worker if one could be found.[24]

The Pioneer Mission was not rich and was unable to pay a worthy wage to the missionaries. Caradoc Jones himself would teach children during the summer months and that gave him an extra £10. He also worked in the garden that provided him with some vegetables and, according to one source, did the gardens of others as well, in order to supplement his income.[25] All the missionaries knew that they had to sacrifice trusting that the settled wages would be paid regularly. Faithful to their call, they lived frugally and were always ready to share amongst themselves.

The workers were paid monthly and details for some periods can be given:[26]

	1947	1957	1958
Rev. C. Jones	£18	£17	£ 20 and 21 given
A. Matthews	£10	£14	£17 and 18 given
Mrs Thompson		£10	£12
Mr Huck	£ 7	£10	No change
Orphanage		5	No change

There was an occasional bonus, like the time when Caradoc Jones and Arthur Matthews received £2-10-0 each. [27] The difficulties are accentuated when the cost of living is borne in mind. A ton of coal cost £15; tea was 25s a pound, meat and butter 7s-6d a pound.[28]

It was natural for all concerned to think of their financial support, but they were more concerned with the progress of the gospel in Paimpol and in Brittany generally. Occasional baptismal services gladdened their hearts. In reporting the baptismal services in 1955, Caradoc Jones also referred to what was happening in Plougrescant, [29] eighteen miles from Paimpol and near 'Plouvouskan hell'. When the wind would whip the waves, local inhabitants believed that they could hear the weeping of the condemned, crying for mercy.[30] The church there had been built by an English lady and was handed over to the Baptist Missionary Society. The Society decided to give up the work and asked Caradoc Jones to be responsible for it. He suggested the Pioneer Mission should be responsible, but that was not possible.

Caradoc Jones agreed to visit and help them in Plougrescant. He was given a car to enable him to travel, 'an old model but workable'.[31]

Conversions were welcomed. Some of the converts were from a Roman Catholic background, some were religious and, occasionally, an atheist would be converted.[32] The colporteur was in contact with such a person and after long discussions with him, he believed the gospel. Such was the rejoicing that the two sang together:[33]

> Thou Heavenly, thou Holy,
> The Lamb without sin;
> From God's Law did save me –
> Its curse and its din;
> Its terrors can't frighten
> My soul any more;
> 'Tis Thee dear Lord Jesus
> Henceforth I'll adore.

Sometimes, Caradoc Jones received a nice surprise as happened in 1960. He received an invitation from the Mayor of Paimpol to a welcome meeting for the Mayor of Romsey.[34] Caradoc Jones had been invited to a meeting by the Mayor of Kerity, but had to refuse the invitation because the particular function was on a Sunday. The pastor attended the meeting at Paimpol and during the proceedings his name was announced with the other guests. The following Sunday morning the mayoral car brought some of the Romseyites to the service that was to be taken by Caradoc Jones. He believed that this had happened as the result of a recent funeral that he had taken. Many people had been impressed by the service.[35]

THE ORPHANAGE

One of those baptized, immediately after Caradoc Jones' return to Paimpol, was the adopted daughter of Miss Cave from the orphanage.[36] Caradoc Jones was glad that they as a church could help the children materially, but it was a cause of greater joy for him when one of them was converted. The work of the orphanage was very dear to him. He would emphasize two aspects of the work. Positively it was an opportunity to make known the love of the Lord Jesus Christ: negatively it was a protest against the Roman Catholic Church and the hold it had over the children.

Included in the reports was the account of a young lad who had just left the orphanage to earn his living as a sailor.[37] He assured the church at Paimpol that, in spite of difficulties, he was making a stand for Christ. He expressed his thanks to the church for its help by sending a small gift. The church was glad to receive such a gift, but there was room for concern as well. The building was in serious need of repair and there was a lack of financial support. At the time, there was a demand for children's homes, not only from Christian circles but also from the government:[38]

> The government, a day or two ago, announced by wireless its need of institutions and homes to open their doors to orphans, and it would pay the cost of their upkeep, and that the children could be brought up in any religion taught at such institutions or homes. Now here is an unprecedented opportunity for us, for the children, for the Gospel faith and for the Kingdom.

Caradoc Jones was not a man to miss such an opportunity.

Although the Government was ready to cover the cost of keeping the children, it would not contribute towards a new building. That depended on the good will of individuals and churches. Help was forthcoming. Miss Cave was willing to lend three or four hundred pounds on mortgage at a low rate, the principal to fall to the Mission at her death and the same sum to purchase a house for an orphanage.[39] Firm promises were received including one gift of a thousand pounds and the church decided to proceed with the project without the help of the Bank of England. Caradoc Jones met the Council in London and reported that 'The Mission at Paimpol had been able to secure the desired property and loans had been raised there to pay for it. Many had lent varying sums of money and one poor woman had changed her loan, which equaled £40, into a gift'.[40]

The orphanage, 'Revenez-Y', was opened 19 June 1947.[41] It was described as a beautiful house with extensive views of the coast. Speakers at the opening were Pastor Somerville, Morlaix, mayor of Kerity and Harry Stamp, who had worked with Caradoc Jones in Vittel. Charles Phillips, the Treasurer, and Winifred M. Pearce represented the Pioneer Mission. Fifty Army blankets had been sent from London, but there was still a need for clothes and shoes. Hope was dampened a little because of the delay in receiving Government grants, and this was the main reason why an extra £125 per annum was needed for the upkeep of the orphanage.[42]

Twelve months after the opening, Miss Cave retired and Mrs Matthews replaced her. Miss Cave was an honorary worker and had given her time, strength and money in the service of the orphanage. The Council suggested that £400 should be laid aside, out of which an annuity would be paid to Miss Cave. The matter was postponed and it is not clear what the Council decided finally.[43] Sometimes, Mrs Matthews received unexpected support. The orphanage did not expect sympathy from the schoolteachers of Brittany. One of them, however, sent a gift to help one of the boys. The gift meant that Joel was able to have shoes, socks and a suit, all costing twenty pounds.[44] After the initial good response, gifts did not flow in, and this meant that it was only possible to take 18-20 orphans, while there was room for twenty-five.

The morning would start with Bible reading and prayer.[45] In the evening some of the children read the French Bible with notes. In the reports from the orphanage, details were given occasionally of the children. A summarized selection will give an idea of what happened to some of them:[46]

Joel, Louisette, Paulette Jean, Francette:	Had done well in different schools. Some of them were ready to go on to higher education
Raymonde:	He works in the home of a Christian surgeon in Paris. Gine, who left the Orphanage ten years ago, found a place for her. Gine worked as a Deaconess in Reuilly Hospital
Jennie:	Is now the wife of Jean L'Heroux, pastor at Angers. The work is being blessed there; a number of Conversions
Georgette:	A Nanny with the Salvation Army
Joel:	Had just started his life as a sailor
Christiane:	Working in Reuilly Hospital, Paris

Care was taken to guide the orphans to a sphere of service.

The orphanage was supported in many different ways. Grants were received from the Mission and the Government, individuals and churches contributed and there was one other way that churches could help. They could adopt a child and be responsible for his keep in the orphanage. One of the churches that did so was Gabalfa Baptist church, Cardiff. It was reported in 1959 that they had been doing so for a number of years.[47] The first orphan that was adopted was Nicole. Her photograph was displayed in the Sunday school every second Sunday in the month. They had also collected for Joel. The Sunday school at Gabalfa and the branch school at Colwill, contributed as much as £140 in one year.[48]

Nicole left the orphanage to be a nurse in Paris and Gabalfa arranged to support two other children. Letters and photographs introduced them to Christian and Marie. They had been introduced to the orphanage by Mr Stamp of St Brieuc. He asked for four children to be taken in, three boys and a girl. The mother had left them to live with another man, and the father had to work, on a low wage, to keep the children. He knew that he could not work and care for the children. Although not orphans, the orphanage received two of them.

Two of the children, Christian and Marie, were accepted into the orphanage, and had been there for six years, before Gabalfa church started to support them.[49]

The orphanage had also given shelter to an invalid, Mlle. Cornec, a faithful member of the church, who was carried to the services in a wheelchair. One of her favourite hymns was the one that echoed 'Here is love vast as the ocean' that was so popular in the 1904-5 Revival in Wales. She died in 1959 at the age of 86 after spending twenty years in the orphanage.[50]

The condition of the old people was a matter of concern for Caradoc Jones. Early in the 1950s he had pleaded with the Council to open a home for old folk. He suggested a small house accommodating five or six people.[51] The Council, although sympathetic, could not respond positively because of its financial situation. The Bank of England would allow money only for missionary work. Furthermore, Charles Phillips had written off the debt on the new orphanage by loan, and there was a need to repay a sum of £60.[52] The answer did not satisfy Caradoc Jones: 'The Council seem to see difficulties on all hands, and so they might where faith does not come in'.[53] Caradoc Jones brought up the matter again in 1960, but it was postponed.

GYPSIES
Gypsies in Europe, even before the Second World War, were classed as second-rate citizens. They were 'non-persons', of 'foreign blood',

and 'labour-shy'.[54] With Jews and homosexuals they faced imprisonment during the war itself and were taken to camps like Warsaw and Lublin, in Poland, and Auschwitz in Germany. Gypsy caravans were compounded. Different figures have been given as to the number of gypsies that died during the war. One estimate is 500,000 but a more conservative estimate is given as 200,000. They died because of ill treatment and hunger and many, by the side of an open grave, were shot naked.[55] When the Vichy Government was formed it made no effort at all to make any changes.

After the war gypsies were still held in suspicion because of the charge of immorality that was aimed at them. The Law demanded that they should not stay in one place for more than twenty-four hours and their children were not allowed to attend school. There were five main groups in France. Some depended on their living by making pegs and baskets, others were tinkers, and one group made carpets and embroidery. This group had quite extensive 'couches' (modern motor car) and visited the markets of France, including Paimpol. It was estimated that 100,000 gypsies were travelling in France during the 1950s.[56]

One Sunday morning, Caradoc Jones was quite surprised to see a number of gypsies coming into the service. They informed him at the end of the service that they were Christians, and that they had been baptized in the sea. A few weeks later, another group attended a meeting and yet another group soon afterwards. [57] On another occasion Caradoc Jones was distributing tracts on the street when he met two gypsy ladies with a baby each in shawls. They asked him about the content of the tracts. When they were told that they presented the message of the Lord Jesus Christ, they responded most enthusiastically. They wanted to know if Caradoc Jones was a pastor and if there was a chapel in the town. They promised to attend a meeting the following Sunday. They kept their word and brought their husbands and children with them, that meant an extra fifteen in the congregation. They attended again the next Sunday.[58]

Two male gypsies passed the chapel and saw the text on the board outside. They went to the Manse to introduce themselves and to inquire concerning the chapel. They were part of a group travelling in fifteen caravans, the majority of whom had been converted. When asked if they could read, they answered in the negative, but added that their people had remarkable memories and could remember conversations and sermons. When asked who preached to the gypsies, one of them said that he did so and that three of his brothers also preached. The company and other companies had a pastor.[59]

A group would have liked to stay for the Sunday but knew very well that they would have to move on before that day. Caradoc Jones was, however, an able persuader and convinced the local authorities that the converted people would not create a disturbance. On the Sunday, a large number attended, filling one side of the chapel while the regular worshippers filled the other side.[60] It was a memorable service, with spontaneous enthusiastic worship, loud praise and open confession of sin, characteristic of a revival meeting in Wales during 1904-5.

It was always easy to recognize a gypsy caravan, but the believers wanted to make clear that theirs belonged to Christians. They painted the sign of the cross, the Bible and a Scripture verse in French on the sides of the caravan. Two visitors to Paimpol, Mr and Mrs Harold Evans, saw such a caravan just before they arrived in the town.[61] When they approached the company, they realized that they had no French and the gypsies could not understand English. The Evanses overcame the problem by taking out their New Testaments, pointed to particular verses, and the gypsies were able to find them in their New Testament. In Paimpol, Caradoc Jones gave more detail concerning these gypsies, including an account of a baptismal service in Paris, when the gypsies baptized four hundred candidates. The gypsies never missed an opportunity to present the teaching on believers baptism by immersion. On one occasion, they persuaded a pastor of the Reformed Church to be baptized. They were anxious to celebrate the occasion, and the gypsies, the pastor and twelve members from Plougrescant, joined together for a time of worship.[62]

Two other groups, one consisting of eight believers and the other consisting of twenty- three believers, came to a Sunday morning communion service. They met around the Lord's Table: 'The unsaved gypsies also attended, but sat apart while the Gypsy, Breton, French and British believers gathered round the Table of the One who invites in one all believers from every race and tongue. It was a happy service'.[63] A number of them were present at the prayer meeting the following Monday. Two of the gypsies had exceptional freedom in prayer: 'Two of the young gypsies, about 18 years of age, prayed with unction, diction and Scriptural and spiritual expression that surprised us, just as if they were students of a Theological College'.[64] Caradoc Jones would visit the Gypsies regularly while they were in the area, and when they were ready to move on to another place, he would meet the company, wish them well and pray with them.

Some groups of gypsies would return a number of times, but one Sunday morning a new group arrived in the chapel. They took their place reverently and listened attentively to the sermon. After the service, they made for the collection box, although no collection had been announced. The elder of the group asked the pastor if he would dedicate one of the children and he agreed to do so that day. In the afternoon service, father and mother, with little Renee Vadoch, who was fifteen days old were called to the front. Caradoc Jones prayed and the congregation recited the verse 'Suffer little children to come to me'. The parents made their vows to the Lord and gave thanks for the child. They, the parents, had been baptized seven years previously.[65] A lasting work of grace was evident in their lives. The gypsies were still attending the church at Paimpol at the end of the 1960s.[66]

155

SUPPORT

In the midst of all his activity, Caradoc Jones would find time to visit supporting churches. There were a number in London, a few in Scotland, a few in north Wales and a strong support in south Wales, especially Cardiff.[67] During October-November 1948, seven meetings were arranged for the missionary in London and he was the guest speaker at a function in Tooting. Eighteen meetings were arranged for him during the 1952 visit, and during his visit to Wales in 1958, Caradoc Jones spoke in eight places.[68] He would also make an effort to be present at the Pioneer Mission Annual Rally at Cardiff usually held in Gabalfa. The congregation there was zealous in their support. They had a representative on the Welsh Auxiliary and on the London Council. Two prominent members on the Council were A. O. Criddle and Harold Evans. Many Criddle families were faithful members in Gabalfa during the ministry of Caradoc Jones. A. O. Criddle was the editor of the *News Bulletin* for many years. Harold Evans was also a member in Gabalfa, but, when he moved to Penarth, joined the Brethren Assembly. Both he and his wife were close friends of Caradoc Jones. In 1960, Arthur T. B. Jones, Gabalfa, became the representative on the Council.

Many older south Wales workers were still active, including D. M. Russell Jones, Gabalfa, and Melville Evans, Gilgal, Porthcawl, and new names appeared in the reports.[69] In north Wales, W. S. Jones, Scotch Baptist elder, and Caradoc's brother supported until his death in 1963. Another elder, J. Hannaby, was also a keen supporter.[70] As to the number of churches in south Wales that supported the Paimpol Mission, there were six or seven that were regular givers and others gave occasionally.[71]

There was a real need for workers in Paimpol itself. Woodside Baptist Church, Norwood, provided two workers before the end of the 1950s. Barry Burton was converted while serving with the British Forces in Berlin. He spent one year at Nogent sur Marne, continuing the link between the College and the church at Paimpol. He also spent one year in All Nations Bible College. His fiancé, Jean Mitchell, was a former student of Redcliffe Missionary Training College. They married and left for Paimpol to concentrate on personal evangelism.[72] There was a need in St Brieuc and that was met for a brief period by Graham Lippet and Gloria, his wife, both from Gabalfa Baptist church, Cardiff. They faced a number of difficulties and were very grateful to Caradoc Jones for all the help they received during that period.[73] Eventually, in 1967, Brian Russell Jones, son of D. M. Russell Jones, the minister of Gabalfa, was appointed to Paimpol.[74]

The appointment was the culmination of long, drawn-out discussions concerning the leadership in Paimpol. A number of possible leaders were mentioned, including David Shepherd, the evangelist from Gorseinon, Swansea, and Graham Lippett, Gabalfa and St Brieuc. The matter of a successor to Caradoc Jones had been mooted as early as 1954, and by 1963 the Council declared that 'It was essential that Mr. Jones be removed from the Field possibly by placing him in the OFH' [Old Folk's Home].[75] There was a need to replace Caradoc Jones, but the Council was rather blunt in dealing with it. They could have considered sending him back to Wales.

Many factors complicated the situation. Caradoc Jones himself was critical of the Council for not acting quickly enough to meet with particular needs. He had invited Harold Evans to be a member of the Council without informing the members. The pastor was also determined to 'die in harness'. There had been misunderstanding concerning the ownership of the property in Paimpol. Members of the Council and some of the members in Paimpol felt that at his age it was not possible for the pastor to respond to all the needs of the work. Some members in Paimpol believed that he had 'out-stayed' his welcome.[76] A further complication was the rumour that was spread concerning the relationship between the pastor and Nurse

Thompson. It had no foundation at all. Nurse Thompson considered legal action, but decided not to proceed, although her family felt strongly that she should have done so.[77]

Caradoc Jones himself was approaching his ninetieth birthday and had also experienced ill health again. He suffered a severe attack of bronchitis and had trouble with his eyes. His stay in Cardiff during 1961 was delayed because he had a cataract removed and, as a result of the operation, had to wear glasses.[78] Two and a half years later he was having breakfast, when, suddenly everything was dark, 'as it were a curtain fall over the eye', that is, the one successfully operated for a cataract.[79] Nurse Thompson advised him to seek a doctor immediately, but he delayed, and when he did reach the doctor it was too late to help him. A surgeon in Cardiff confirmed that that it was a case of 'thrombosis at the back of the eye'. It was possible to remove a cataract from the other eye.[80]

LEAVING DEAR OLD PAIMPOL

Matters came to a head in 1966. The Council decided[81]

> To implement the decision to retire the Rev. C. Jones, it was AGREED: that Mr. Moxham and Mr. Cliff go to Paimpol at the end of May with powers to adapt the foregoing decisions [retirement Caradoc Jones and other matters discussed in the Council] in the light of discussions held.

Caradoc Jones knew that the end had come and that it would not be possible for him to 'die in harness'. It was not until 1967 that he left his dear old Paimpol. The Chairman of the Pioneer Mission paid tribute to him:[82]

> Over the years his ministry has been self-sacrificing and whole hearted. He went to Brittany at an age when most men are well advanced in their ministries. Now, forty-seven years later, we salute him on his retirement.

Others, including Graham Lippett, paid tribute to him in the *News Bulletin*.

The farewell service was held 28 May 1967 and it was in May 1920 that he had left for Paimpol the first time. Several ministers spoke in the meeting and expressed their high regard for Caradoc Jones. An elder, Louis le Roux, spoke on behalf of the congregation and did so with much emotion. Madame Berthos spoke on behalf of the believers at Plougrescant. A number of those who had been in the orphanage, including some from Paris, returned to share in the farewell meeting. Others who could not attend sent their greetings.

It is significant that one of the hymns sang in the meeting was 'Torrents d'amour et de grâce' that echoed the English version 'Here is love vast as the ocean' by William Edwards, Cardiff. That version was a translation of the Welsh original, 'Dyma gariad fel y moroedd', by William Rees, 'Gwilym Hiraethog'). The author of the French version was Reuben Saillens, well known to Caradoc Jones. Both of them had been present at meetings in the Metropolitan Tabernacle and the College during the Revival of 1904-5. Caradoc had sung the hymn as a member of the Welsh Quartette and Saillens had sung his own version of the hymn to the tune 'Ebeneser'. The relationship was renewed when Caradoc Jones went to Brittany in 1920, although they could have met in different Baptist meetings during the Welshman's ministry in Cardiff. Caradoc Jones was able to follow the three versions of the hymn. It also reminded him of the Revival and helped to keep alive the hope for another spiritual awakening.

Caradoc Jones and Nurse Thompson left from St Brieuc Airport for London the Wednesday after the farewell meeting. The Rev. Brian Russell-Jones followed Caradoc Jones in Paimpol. As mentioned above he was the son of D. M. Russell-Jones, minister of Gabalfa Baptist church, Cardiff, where the leaving missionary had ministered form 1907 until 1920.

1. 'Back again at Paimpol', *The Pioneer Review,* April-June, 1946.
2. Ibid.
3. Ibid., Charles Phillips, 'A visit o Brittany', July-December, 1946.
4. 'Back again at Paimpol', April-June, 1946.
5. Ibid.
6. Angus Library, Council Meeting, 21 November 1951, 9.
7. Ibid., 13 April 1949, 134.
8. Ibid., 9 September, 136.
9. 'News from the field', *The Pioneer Review,* October-December, 1963.
10. Angus Library, Council Meeting, 24 March 1950, 141.
11. Ibid., 21 October 1950, 144.
12. Ibid., 9 September 1949, 136.
13. Interview with Sylvia Le Saux, Pierre's widow, Reading.
14. Ibid.
15. Ibid.
16. Ibid.
17. Ibid.
18. Ibid, interview Havard and Rhiannon Gregory, Cardiff.
19. Interview Havard and Rhiannon Gregory, Cardiff.
20. The Old Catholic Church: One characteristic of the Church was the emphasis on reading the Bible. The leader was von Döllinger (1799-1890): J. D. Douglas, ed. *The New Dictionary of the Christian Church* (Paternoster, 1974).
21. Interview Sylvia Le Saux, Reading.
22. Copy of letter, 23 April 1966, from Sylvia Le Saux, Reading. In writing to Pierre, 15 November 1967, Caradoc Jones referred to the fact that he had just been to the funeral of the missionary, Winifred Davies, Coedpoeth, who was martyred in the Congo.
23. Angus Library, Council Meeting, 3 June 1955, 66.
24. Ibid., 24 September 1948, 129.
25. Interview Sylvia Le Saux, Reading.
26. Angus Library, Council Meeting, 18 July 1958, 128; 24 September 1958, 130.
27. Ibid., 26 November 1962, 184.
28. Ibid., Scrap Book, cutting from *The Christian,* 14 November 1952.
29. Ibid., Council Meeting, 4 November 1955, 80.
30. Gwyn Griffiths, *Crwydro Llydaw,* 204.
31. Angus Library, Council Meeting, 4 November 1955, 80.
32. 'The conversion of an atheist', *The Pioneer Review,* May-June, 1961.
33. Ibid.
34. Ibid., 'Was it a sequel?', July-August, 1960.
35. Ibid. Michael McGowan informs the author that: 'Paimpol and Romsey are now twinned within the European scheme of twinning towns from various countries'.
36. Ibid., 'Back again at Paimpol', April-June, 1946.
37. Ibid.

38. Ibid.
39. Angus Library, Council Meeting, 21 June 1946, 96.
40. Ibid., 7 November 1946, 102; 10 January 1947, 185.
41. Ibid., 30 May 1947, 111, includes cutting, 'Evangelizing Brittany's Children', from *The Christian*, 10 July 1947.
42. Ibid., 9 July 1947, 114.
43. Ibid., 23 April 1948, 126.
44. 'News from the field', *The Pioneer Review*, January-February, 1959.
45. *News Bulletin*, May-June, 1956.
46. 'News from the field'. *The Pioneer Review*, January-February, 1959; ibid. 'They were once at the Orphanage', January-February, 1960.
47. *News Bulletin*, November-December, 1959.
48. Ibid.
49. Ibid.
50. 'Mlle Le Conec', *The Pioneer Review*, July-August, 1959.
51. Angus Library: 'Old Folk's Homes', Council Meeting, 30 September 1953, 38
52. Ibid., 10 March 1954.
53. Ibid., 7 May 1954.
54. 'On Gypsies' – The Cybrary of Holocaust, viewed 15/07/2004.
55. Ibid. Also, study of Gypsies in France: Open Directory-Society-Ethnicity, viewed 16/07/2004
56. Ibid.
57. Caradoc Jones, 'Y Sipsiwn i Grist', *Rhos Herald*, 10 September 1955.
58. Ibid.
59. Ibid., 17 September 1955.
60. *Knight in Royal Service*, 45.
61. Angus Library: 'Report of my visit to Paimpol'. Typed account by Mrs W. Harold Evans.
62. Ibid. Mr Hunter, Field Director, visited Paimpol: 'Mr Hunter found that the gypsies are persecuted by the police but he had the joy of holding a service in one of their caravans', Council Meeting, 14 September 1956.
63. *Pioneer Review*, Summer 1957.
64. Ibid.
65. 'Mademoiselle Renee Vadoch', *The Pioneer Review*, November – December, 1958.
66. Ibid., e.g. 'The Gypsies', July-September, 1966. The early 1950s in France witnessed a wide range spiritual revival amongst the gypsies that led to the movement 'Light and Life'. In fifty years time it was still strong: e.g. 15,000 gypsies gathered for a rally in 2002. They were described as 'Protestant and evangelical', Two New Gypsies Granted Asylum in France, viewed 12/10/06.
67. During his October-November 1948 tour, he visited the following churches: Hetherfield Road, Streatham; Walworth Road; Tabernacle, Uxbridge Road; Chatsworth, Norwood; North Road Baptist, Brentford; Tooting Junction, and Kingston Baptist: Angus Library, Council Meeting:

24 September 1948, 129; he had 18 engagements in and around London during his November 1952 visit, ibid., 5 November 1952, 23; Cardiff: 24 September 1948, 129; 30 September 1953, 35.

68. Ibid., 'Itinerary', 5 November 1952, 23; 'Visit of Caradoc Jones', *The Pioneer Review*, March-April, 1958.
69. Harold Evans and A. T. B Jones from Gabalfa Baptist, Cardiff; Rev. Paul Tucker, Barry; David Shepherd, the evangelist, Gorseinon.
70. W. S. Jones, Caradoc Jones' brother and J. Hannaby, Rhos were staunch supporters; both of them Scotch Baptist leaders.
71. Some of the regular givers: Gabalfa English Baptist; Splott Road English Baptist; Longcross English Baptist; Tabernacle Welsh Baptist, in Cardiff; Princes Street Mission, Barry; Bethany Hall, Penarth, and Caersalem Welsh Baptist, Llanelli.
72. Angus Library, Council Meeting, 7 July 1959, 140; 1 April 1960, 1449; *Knight in Royal Service*, 47.
73. Council Meeting, 27 May 1964, 12; 2 September 1964, 15.
74. Paimpol Archive, Michel Le Garsmeur, 'The Story of the Baptist Church in Paimpol, Brittany', 14.
75. Angus Library, Council Meeting, 11 January 1963, 186.
76. Ibid., 18 May 1967, 62.
77. Interview Sylvia Le Saux, Reading.
78. Angus Library, Council Meeting, 3 February 1961, 160.
79. 'That Dark Night', *The Pioneer Review*, July-September, 1963.
80. Ibid.
81. Angus Library, Council Meeting, 18 May 1966.
82. 'Retirement in his Ninety-third', *News Bulletin*, April-June, 1967.

9

LAST DAYS AND RESPONSE

Caradoc Jones returned to Rhos, Wrexham, and settled with some of his relatives. Nurse Thompson also returned from Paimpol but worked for one year in Holloway Prison. The money she earned during that period was given as a contribution towards buying a house for Caradoc Jones in Rhos, and she kept house for him.[1] They settled in 'Llydaw', New Street, Rhos.

It was only for about eighteen months that Caradoc Jones enjoyed his stay in Rhos. He passed away on 12 January 1969 and was buried in Rhos Cemetery, three days later. A large number attended the funeral, when tributes were paid to the missionary during the services in the home and in the chapel. They were characterized by praise to God for all his goodness. The Rev. Ridley Williams, Mount Pleasant Baptist, led the service in the home and the Rev. Lewis Valentine, Penuel Welsh Baptist, led the service in Mount Pleasant. A number of people took part, including Brian Russell-Jones and Arthur Matthews from Brittany. Representatives were present from a wide area, including Paimpol and Cardiff.[2]

APPRECIATION

Caradoc Jones gained the admiration of many in Wales, England, especially London, Scotland and France. He was a friendly character. Some would say that he was too serious, while others would say that he had a sense of humour. The response depended on the closeness of the friendship. He could establish a good relationship even with those that disagreed with him, including Roman Catholic priests.

Caradoc Jones' mind and spirit had been well prepared for service even before he started on his public ministry. He was thirty-two years of age when he started his ministry in Gabalfa, Cardiff. By that time, the home, the Scotch Baptists, his experience in the shop, college and revival had molded his character.

No one can doubt Caradoc Jones' courage and determination. He decided to leave the Scotch Baptists on the ground of conviction. He was one of the leaders in the College Mission in London. His evangelistic zeal led to the building of a new chapel in Gabalfa. The BMS advised him not to go to Brittany. Caradoc Jones, however, was convinced that God was calling him, not only to Brittany, but specifically to Paimpol. The conviction was not purely subjective because it was confirmed by the Pioneer Mission and acknowledged by the Gabalfa church in Cardiff. The determination and courage were especially evident during the two periods of internment. When he decided to return to Paimpol in 1946, Caradoc Jones was 71 years old.

Brittany was only a few hours' journey from the south of England. It was easy for Caradoc Jones to keep in touch with his supporters and they were able to keep in touch with him. Consequently, the supporters could cross to Paimpol and spend periods of time working with him. It was an unusual missionary arrangement. He often expressed appreciation of all the help that he received. Caradoc Jones also had co-workers in Paimpol and was very indebted to them, but the burden of the work was on the Welshman's shoulders and that burden seemed to increase regularly. Later in his ministry, however, he was reluctant to delegate work, especially to the younger workers. This attitude made it more difficult for them to settle in Paimpol.

Caradoc Jones was an enthusiastic evangelist and caring pastor. He combined the emphasis on personal salvation with the emphasis on the church as a gathered community. This was true of his work, not only in Gabalfa, Cardiff, but during internment as well. He was also concerned with the material and emotional needs of others, especially the children and the elderly. His ministry was not confined to the respectable of society; it extended to those living on the fringes of society. Many groups of gypsies in Paimpol were grateful for his patient ministry. At times the growth of the work at Paimpol was slow, while at other times there were real encouragements. Whatever the situation, Caradoc Jones was given persevering grace. The work, pioneered by Terrell, was confirmed and expanded during the ministry of Caradoc Jones. When he left, it was possible for the church to be independent and it continues to this day to bear witness to the gospel faithfully proclaimed by Caradoc Jones.

The missionary to Brittany was content to minister in a small mission field, irrespective of rewards for himself. During the war he had seen many military leaders decorated with medals and applauded for their bravery. Caradoc Jones received no medals and was often criticized and not applauded. As a believer, he knew that the medals could not be compared to the crown laid up for those who love the appearing of the Lord Jesus Christ. (2 Tim. 4: 8).

Working in Brittany, Caradoc Jones had to learn Breton as well as French. As a warm hearted Welshman he would have been glad to do so. He did not, however, make an attempt to form a Breton cause. That would have been possible, in spite of restrictions, when he arrived in 1920, especially in the Plouha area. He was also a Baptist, accepting believer's baptism by immersion. The emphasis on the ordinance could be so strong, it tended to become a major matter, rather than a secondary one. His Welsh Nonconformist background could influence him in matters of discipline. He could be rather negative in his approach. According to one of his critics, Caradoc Jones frowned on legitimate exercise, like tennis. In Wales, during the same period, many would regard kicking a ball as sinful as being drunk.

Doctrinally, Caradoc Jones modified the Calvinism of his

background. One influence that led to that change was John Fletcher of Madeley. Sometimes the emphasis on man's responsibility before God can give the impression that man has the ability to respond to the call of the gospel. Caradoc Jones made use of decision cards, but there is no evidence that he pressurized people to believe the gospel. He acknowledged the central place of the Holy Spirit in conversion and sanctification.

It is a pity that Caradoc Jones did not leave Paimpol before 1967. This was his greatest mistake. He had been so wise most of the time, but once he determined to 'die in harness' it opened up the way for unpleasantness. Leaving a few years earlier would have avoided tension and misunderstanding.

ISSUES

SUFFERING: Suffering always creates problems and prompts questions. Horrible atrocities happen during a time of war and many ask Where is God? or, On whose side is he? The suicide bombings in London, 2005, led to the death of over fifty people and injured many hundreds, making the suffering of the innocent a stark reality. It is possible to suffer at the hands of others; it is possible to bring suffering on ourselves while at other times there is no obvious reason for the suffering. The internees at Besançon and Vittel were painfully aware of man's inhumanity to man. Most of them did not suffer to the same degree as those in the concentration camps, but there was suffering. They suffered physically because of lack of food. They suffered emotionally because of being confined, especially those who were separated from loved ones and had no idea where they were located. The hotels were overcrowded. People lived on top of each other, which led to personal tensions and opened up the way to immorality. The Jews experienced extreme cruelty at the hands of the Germans, and hundreds were taken from Besançon and Vittel to concentration camps. Furthermore, they had no idea how long they would be interned. Uncertainty and fear drained their spiritual resources very often.

What was the response in the internment camp? A few managed to escape. The situation was too much for a number of people and they responded by committing suicide, while others lost their reason. On the other hand the response in the camp reveals the resolute nature of man's spirit. The fighting spirit is in man as a created being. Furthermore he can reflect his Creator in being creative. There was much creative activity in the camp that was therapeutic in nature. It is surprising how many painters and musicians were interned, while the women had pleasure in their sewing. Creative work was always therapeutic, but a painting, for example, presented to the guard, could also be a means of having more bread. It was also possible to keep a diary. This would keep the mind active, and the diary could be taken out later to provide information regarding the condition of the camp. The Jews responded by safeguarding their religion and national traditions. This was made possible because they were interned together in one place.

Caradoc Jones and the believers under his care responded in a Christian context. They came together to worship, realizing that their God was with them. They were in fellowship where they could minister the one to the other. They were never alone, which was a source of strength for all of them. Caradoc Jones himself exercised his gifts of singing, composing and personal witness. Instead of turning in upon himself, he gave all that he had in order to serve others.

The missionary from Rhos was continually reminded of the possibilities of sin and evil. On the one hand he could admire the beauty of the work of an artist, while on the other hand he would see Jews being dragged away to be put to death like animals. He knew that he was working in a fallen world. C. S. Lewis argued that Christ took it for granted that men are bad: 'Until we really feel this assumption of his to be true, though we are part of the world he came to save, we are not part of the audience to whom his words are addressed'.[3] This is an essential aspect of the believer's world-view.

C. S. Lewis also says that it was to this fallen world that Christ came to save sinners, Jews and Gentiles.[4] It was in Christ that the love of God was manifested to respectable sinners like Caradoc Jones and to evil men like Hitler and Himmler. This is another aspect of the believer's world-view. God is not the author of sin, but he has done everything necessary to deal with it, and that once and for all, in the Lord Jesus Christ. The experience of forgiveness bears fruit in a forgiving spirit. Caradoc Jones was ill treated by the German soldiers, but when he faced them after returning to Paimpol there was forgiveness and compassion in his heart.

Like the persons of faith in Hebrews, chapter 11, it was by faith that Caradoc Jones persevered in France. It is no surprise at all for a man who had known illness and suffering to tell his friend, Pierre, to turn for comfort to the Book of Job and Romans, chapter 8. Faith, when tried, is purified like gold in the fire. It is proved to be genuine and will result in praise and honour when Jesus Christ will be revealed (1 Peter 1:7), and compare 1 John 5: 4-5. Faith looks, not to the things that are visible but to the things that are invisible. Faith can look into the future when sin and evil will be removed. Faith is also essential for a truly Christian world-view.

MISSION: Caradoc Jones persevered in an entrenched Roman Catholic country. He was a strong opponent of that Church and fought strenuously to withstand its influence. He regarded his main task as evangelism, that is, to win the Roman Catholics to the faith of the gospel. He would not consider the charge that he was proselytizing. It was enough for him that the Scriptures proclaimed Christ as the unique Son of the Father. Here was God's final word to a sinful world. Caradoc Jones did not live long enough to witness the impact of the Second Vatican, because it did not come to an end until

1965. His friend, Pierre, was more optimistic concerning the Roman Catholic Church. He welcomed any sign of reformation within its ranks, while Caradoc Jones would emphasize the unchanging nature of the church, that is, as far as the basic teaching was concerned.

The conflict continues. It is the conflict between evangelical and sacramental grace. It is the conflict between the authority of the Word of God and the authority of the Church and Tradition. It is the conflict between the belief that Jesus Christ is the unique Son of God and any religion that denies that uniqueness. It was the unique Christ that accomplished the only salvation through his death on the Cross. Caradoc Jones, like Paul, knew nothing among the people but 'Christ crucified'. This was the message that burned in his bones. In the temple, on the street, in a home or on a ship, his message was always the same. It is proper to remember him as one of the internees thought of him after the liberation of Vittel: 'I can still see his grave, sweet face explaining Christ's great sacrifice'.[5] The great, finished sacrifice was the basis of everything that Caradoc Jones did. He knew that, because of the finished work of the cross, nothing could prevent the continuing work of the gospel.

1. Interview Sylvia de Soux.,Reading.
2. 'The Rev. C. Jones, Rhos', *Wrexham Leader*, 24 January 1969.
3. C. S. Lewis, *The Problem of Pain* (Fontana Books, 1957), 45.
4. Ibid. chapter 111.
5. Chapter 7, reference 37.

INDEX

172

Pentyrch Street, Cathays, 52, 53, 55, 56, 58
Penydarren, Merthyr, 33,40
Phillips, Charles, 61, 80-1, 88, 89, 90, 92, 150, 152
Phillips, Thomas, 35-6
Pierce, Samuel, 23
Pierce, Winifred, 125, 126, 150
Pierre le Saux, 143-6, 168, 169
Pioneer Mission, the, 44, 45, 46, 61, 63-4, 67, 68, 73, 103, 113, 135, 146-7, 156, 158, 164
    Women's Auxiliary, 84, 97, 105
Pioneer Review, The, 70, 77, 89, 127, 141
Ploubazlanec, 68
Plouezec, 67, 72
Plougrescant, 100, 147-8, 159
Plouha, 72, 100, 104-5
Plourivo, 67, 72,
Ponciau, 11, 13, 35, 37, 113, 135
Pontfadog Scotch Baptist church, 11, 22, 23, 25
Pontnewydd, 33
Pontrieux, 67, 72
Pontycymer, 42
Pontypridd, 40
Porthmadog, 25
Pullen, H. H., 116, 117, 118

Ramoth, 16, 17, 18, 19
Rechabites, 59
Redcliffe Missionary Training College, 157
Rees, William (Gwilym Hiraethog), 159
Rent Heavens, 142
Rhosllannerchrugog (Rhos), 11-16, 19, 20, 21, 23, 24, 34-5, 135-6, 163
    Tabernacle Scotch Baptist, 23, 25, 35
Rhos Herald, 12, 35
Richardson, Evan, 17
Roberts, Evan, 34, 36, 39, 40
Roberts, J. E., 57
Roberts, Robert (Clynnog), 17
Roberts, Robert (Rhos-ddu), 17, 20
Ropars, Mademoiselle, 93
Ruabon, 38
Rumney, 51, 58
Ruthin, 19, 20

Saillens, Reuben, Dr, 44-5, 46, 60, 63, 71, 72, 159
Sandeman, Robert, 17
Schorr, Professor, 125
Scotch Baptists, 11, 16-23, 35
Scotch Baptist teaching, 17-18
Shepherd, David, 157
Soar Scotch Baptist church, see under Aberderfyn, Ponciau
Society of Friends, 67
Somerville, Pastor (Tremel), 90